Pirana

Pharmacometrics workbench for NONMEM & PsN

Installation guide
Manual
Tutorial
Quick Guides

Pirana version ≥ 2.9.1

1

Contents

II Tutorial: Pirana, PsN & Xpose   74

III Quick guides   100

Chapter 1

Introduction

Pirana is a modeling workbench for NONMEM, PsN and Xpose, offering a graphical user interface and many auxiliary tools to support modeling & simulation analyses.

Development of Pirana was started in 2007, and development still continues. Pirana is currently released under a commercial license for non-academic users, while it is released (free of charge) under a Creative Commons license for academic users. For the detailed license, please see the license document supplied with each Pirana version.

Pirana is designed to be very flexible, and extendible: it integrates with many existing software such as R, Excel, and Berkeley Madonna, and it runs on all major operating systems. We aim for Pirana to be very intuitive, but browsing through this manual before you start working with Pirana is recommended. For many common functionality in Pirana, a Quick Guide is available (from Pirana's help-menu, or from www.pirana-software.com). Also have a look at our website for more information and an FAQ.

Please note that since 2014, a web-version of Pirana is also available: *PiranaJS*. The aim of this web-app is to provide a fast and easily accessible modeling workbench for use on clusters and in the cloud. PiranaJS is released under the same commercial and academic licenses, more information is available on our website.

This booklet includes the Pirana manual

Please do not hesitate to contact us if you have any questions about Pirana or any of the other tools developed by us.

info@pirana-software.com

Part I

Pirana manual

Chapter 2

Pirana installation

Software requirements are summarized below, followed by some additional details on the installation procedure.

2.1 Required / recommended software

Although the only real requirement is an installation of NONMEM, some additional software is highly recommended for optimal use of Pirana, while other softwares might be useful as well.

NONMEM Pirana can use both standard 'from-CD'-installation of NONMEM and NMQual NONMEM installations. NONMEM doesn't have to be installed on your local PC, since Pirana can also connect to other PCs or clusters.

R This open-source software can be obtained from http://www.r-project.org/, and is highly recommended for optimal use of Pirana. R Studio (http://www.r-studio.org/) is a powerful GUI for R that works well with Pirana. Severall R libraries need to be installed to be able to use all the R scripts that are included in the Scripts library in Pirana, such as: lattice, ggplot2, MASS.

PsN Strictly, Pirana does not require PsN installed, although the PsN-toolkit is highly recommended. The latest version of PsN can be obtained from http://psn.sourceforge.net/.

Xpose This R-package for model diagnostics is recommended and can be obtained from http://xpose.sourceforge.net. An Xpose GUI is available within Pirana.

WFN Not required/recommended. Pirana offers only basic support for Wings for NONMEM.

NMQual Recommended for keeping an audit trail of NM installations and autamatically performing bug-fixes. Pirana supports the use of NMQual NONMEM installations. NMQual also requires Perl and the module XML::XPath installed. More details can be found at the Metrum website

2.2   Installation

2.2.1   Installation procedure on Windows

Download the installer from the Pirana website, and install to any location on your hard-drive. Before exploring Pirana's functions, you should first check your settings (*File → Settings → General...*) and software integration (*File → Settings → Software locations...*). If you want to connect to clusters, also update the *Cluster* settings. Pirana is tested on XP, Vista, 7, and 8. Upon installation, Windows or a virus scanner may complain that installation is not safe, but this warning can be ignored, we make every effort to provide virus-free software.

2.2.2   Installation procedure on Mac OS X

On Mac, you should first install the Xcode tools, which are included as optional installs on the (Snow) Leopard install DVDs. In the most recent OSX versions, Xcode can be installed from the App Store. After installing Xcode, make sure you also install the Command Line Tools (From within Xcode, go to *Preferences*, and *Downloads*). Secondly you will have to install an X-window manager. For old versions of OSX, X11 is most likely already installed. If you are running Lion or later, you will however have to install XQuartz instead of X11, which is downloadable online (google for 'XQuartz').

Pirana for Mac is distributed as an executable, so no Perl installation is required, but it is also possible to run from source (see Linux explanation). When opening Pirana for the first time, your system may complain that Pirana is not safe, since it is not installed from the App Store. In this case, you will have to set your security settings in your systems *Preferences* to run apps from *Everywhere*, instead of from *App Store only*.

11

2.2.3   Installation procedure on Linux

For Linux, an executable is made available as well. This executable is compiled on a 32-bit system. If for some reason this executable doesn't run on your system, the Perl source-code can be executed directy in Perl. This requires manual installation of a few additional libraries and modules, see below.

Installing Perl and X11 development libraries

For Pirana to be able to create the GUI, the X11 development libraries (libX11-dev) should be installed, as well as the Perl/Tk module. In Ubuntu / Debian, you can use the Synaptic package manager to install these, or using apt from the shell:

```
sudo apt-get install libX11-dev perl-tk
```

Installing additional Perl modules

Pirana makes use of a number of publicly available Perl-modules, which should also be installed. Some of these modules are likely to be already installed with you current Perl distribution, while others have to be installed manually. Below is a short guidance on how to install these modules. Further guidance on installing Perl modules can be found here: http://www.cpan.org/modules/INSTALL.html). To make a connection to the Perl module archive (CPAN), type:

```
sudo perl -MCPAN -e shell
```

The following commands may be needed to set up the CPAN shell to be able to correctly make the modules into your Perl distribution.

```
o conf make /usr/bin/make
o conf make_install_make_command 'sudo make'
o conf commit
```

Next, use the install command to install required modules into your Perl distribution (mind the case-sensitivity for the module names). Look in Some of these may already be installed, which will be reported as such. If you cannot install some modules from CPAN directly, you have to download and install these modules (and their dependencies) manually. Look in the file pirana.pl to see which modules to install (this may change between Pirana versions).

```
install Tk::PlotDataset
install Tk::JComboBox
install ...
```

Some required modules cannot be installed directly from CPAN. These modules are supplied with Pirana (in the folder /packages) and should be installed manually. From within each of the two package folders, execute in a shell:

```
perl Makefile.PL
make
sudo make install
```

Note: Checking whether Perl modules are installed correctly can be done by executing the following in the terminal window, e.g.: perl -e 'use Tk' which should result in no error messages.

Pirana installation

After installing these Perl modules, copy the entire pirana folder contained in the zip-file to e.g. your home folder (/home/username/) or /opt/pirana/ if you are system admin. Make sure that all perl files in that folder have execution rights. To grant these rights to yourself you can execute the following in the shell from within the Pirana folder:

```
sudo chmod 711 -R *
```

Pirana execution

Pirana can now be started from the command line using

```
perl pirana.pl
```

from within the Pirana folder. Pirana was tested on Ubuntu (9.04-12.04), OpenSUSE (11.1), and Arch Linux, with various Perl distributions. Pirana should work on any Linux distribution with X-windows and Perl/Tk installed.

2.3 Installation of license file

License files can be installed by going to *Help → Import license file*. On Windows, you can also install the license file by dropping it on the

Pirana main window. Upon starting Pirana, the presence of a valid license file (pirana.lic) in Pirana's main installation folder will be checked. If no valid license file is present, a message will be displayed and some functionality of Pirana will be disabled. Academic, commercial, or trial license files can be obtained on the website.

2.4 Configuration

Although most preferences will be correct by default, we recommend to check at least the settings detailed below. Familiarize yourself with the other options as well, to get the most out of Pirana. Especially check the correct file extensions for NONMEM model files and output files.

File extension of models NONMEM control streams/model files. Default is .mod. Note that multiple model file extensions can be specified separated by a comma, e.g. mod,ctl.

File extension of results NONMEM output. Default is .lst

Software settings Pirana needs to know where other important software is installed, which is specified under *Software* from the *File* menu. References to software that you do not have installed, may be disregarded as they are ignored by Pirana.

Code editor Preferably an editor syntax-highlighting. We recommend the use of Emacs (all OS), Sublime Text 2/3 (all OS), PSPad (Windows), ConTEXT (Windows). If none is entered, or a non-existing program is specified, Pirana will use its built-in NM-TRAN editor.

R location The location (folder) of R, e.g. C:/Program Files/R/R-3.1.0. On Windows, at first start-up of Pirana it will search for the latest version of R that is installed, and automatically updates this setting accordingly. If R is installed in a non-standard location, please update this.

R GUI The GUI to be used for R-scripts. Recommended for this is RStudio or Emacs/ESS, but the RGUI supplied with the R distribution can also be used.

spreadsheet The location of your spreadsheet application, e.g. Excel or Gnumeric. Pirana tries to find your spreadsheet automatically.

Note: on Mac OSX you can either specify the application name (e.g. "Microsoft Excel"), or the actual location of the application (e.g. `/usr/local/bin/emacsclient`).

2.5 Configuration for modeling groups

IT sysadmins that want to distribute Pirana to a modeling group with pre-specified settings can do so by editing the files in the folder ini_defaults before distributing Pirana. This will allow users to start with appropriate defaults for Pirana's setting. Also, one or more clusters can be added by default, so that users do not have to add these themselves (and only have to update their username and login). Look in the file /ini_defaults/clusters/readme.txt for further information.

Configuration files location

If even more control is required, i.e. if the end-user should not be allowed to change part of the configuration at all, it is possible to change the location of the configuration files from the user's home directory to a different, protected shared location. The default location for Pirana's configuration files can be overriden by using the file ini_locations.ini located in the folder where you installed Pirana. Change the central ini-files rights to read-only, to be sure users do not change the central settings. More information about how to use this functionality is available in the annotated ini_locations.ini file itself.

Chapter 3

Using Pirana

3.1 Overview

3.1.1 Basic functions

The Pirana window consists of a large area showing an overview of models in the current folder, and a smaller area on the right. The main overview acts as an *electronic lab-notebook* for modeling analyses. The list on the right shows e.g. datasets, R-scripts, or all files in the active folder, or alternatively a list of parameter estimates or reports, or a list of Git/SVN commits. Most buttons in Pirana's main screen are accompanied by a short description which is displayed if hovered above with the mouse pointer. By selecting a model or (data-) file in either lists and right-clicking the mouse, a menu with actions on models or run results is shown. Most of Pirana's functionality is available from this menu, and most options are also available from the toolbar (*View → Show toolbar*).

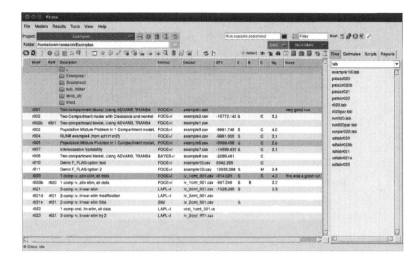

Figure 3.1: Pirana main screen (on Linux)

3.1.2 Model management

The main model overview is where all models and subdirectories in the current working directory are displayed. Only models are displayed that have a file-extension corresponding to the file extension specified in the *preferences*. If multiple file extensions were specified, choose the one you want to use in the current folder by selecting it from the listbox (the one next to the folder selector, on the right above the main models list). When models are double-clicked, the control stream is opened in the code-editor (if specified), or else in Pirana's built-in NM-TRAN editor.

Model views

By default, the model overview is shown as a list, listing all models ordered by run number. It is advised, but not mandatory, that models are named as a number (e.g. 001.mod), or prepended with run (e.g. run1.mod, or run001.mod), see *Conventions and Methods* for more information. By default, the list is shown in *condensed mode*, meaning that for every model, a single row is used in the table. The list can however also be shown in *expanded mode*, which allows for longer model descriptions and notes in the overview. Additionally, in this mode all estimation methods are shown, while in condensed mode

19

only the last estimation method and associated OFV is shown.

An alternate view mode is *tree view*, in which model development is shown as a hierarchical tree. The tree is built using parent/reference information included in the model files (see 'run record' explanation in this manual). When creating models in Pirana, this information is added automatically, and adheres to PsN's run record syntax.

The columns that are shown in the main overview can be activated or de-activated from the *View → Show columns* menu. Models can be filtered using the 'Filter' above the main overview table, or by colors or flags.

Model actions

New models can be created from scratch, from a template, by using the Wizards, or by duplicating an existing model:

Wizards Models can be created by using the PK model wizard. Choose the desired model type and estimation method, and a basic NONMEM model file will be created.

Templates Many basic template models are included. It is possible to build your own library with base models that you often use. Templates can be added by copying a model file to /templates in the Pirana directory. The template models should have the same file extension as your model files to be recognized as a template.

Duplication Duplication of models can be performed by selecting the parent model and clicking 'duplicate' from the context-menu (right click on the model). Optionally, final parameter estimates from the reference model can be updated in the new model, and also model-file numbers in $TABLE and $EST records. Some basic syntax rules should be adhered to ensure correct interpretation of final estimates, see Conventions and Methods at the end of this chapter. A model can also be *Duplicated for MSF restart*. This means that the model file is duplicated, but an $MSFI record is added, parameter estimate blocks are commented out, and the $MSFO record is updated.

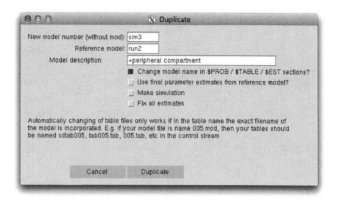

Figure 3.2: Duplicate model

Automated modeling workflow From version 2.10.0, an *automated modeling workflow* is available in Pirana, in which models can be generated from a library. The aim of this functionality is to streamline the analysis of a new dataset, by fitting a range of models to it. This functionality is explained in more detail in a separate section.

Notes, flags and colors

To each model or run in Pirana, you can attach notes, flags, and colors. The colors can indicate e.g. *key runs*, *good runs*, or *bad runs*, but of course the meaning of the flags and color-coding is all up to the user. The notes and color info are stored in a database file (*pirana.dir*), which is created automatically in each folder that holds models. To add notes to a model, select the model, right click and select *Model → Notes and info*, or using the *Ctrl-I* shortcut. Models and results can be given a color by selecting the model, right-clicking, and selecting the desired color/flag from the *Colors & flags* submenu. Pirana also supports filtering of models/runs by color.

Note: In each active folder that is visited with Pirana, a small SQLite database is created ('pirana.dir') which is able to store information about models. So if you archive your projects manually, make sure to include these files as well.

3.1.3 Projects

Pirana allows you to save a link to a folder as a project, which will then be shown in the blue optionmenu (above the active folder entry). This allows you to quickly switch to the directory that is linked to that project. To add a project to the list, browse to a folder by clicking on the folder-icon next to the location bar, or by clicking through the directory-listing in the model overview. Next, click on the *disk*-icon next to the project name, give your project a unique name and press *Save*. Your project is now available from the listbox. To delete a project from the list, click the trash icon next to the project list. The green refresh-icon refreshes the view of the current directory, and should be applied when you make changes to models or add files outside of Pirana. Also when a run is finished, you should refresh to gather the results into Pirana.

3.1.4 Data files

The list on the right of the screen shows files in the current folder, if *Files* is selected as the active tab. Pirana can show tab-files, csv-files, R scripts, Xpose files, and other files, which can be selected from the list above. It is also possible to specify your own filter. Right-clicking on a selected file shows a menu with possible actions on the file.

Note: When the Xpose option is chosen, only unique run numbers are shown, instead of all tabualar data files. After selecting an Xpose dataset, click the 'Open in R' the right-click-menu, and R read in the datasets and create the Xpose object.

3.2 Working with NONMEM

There are several ways in which NONMEM can be used from Pirana. The first one is to use the `nmfe`-script supplied with NONMEM. For this, you have to instruct Pirana where NONMEM is installed. The other (recommended) way to run NONMEM, is to use PsN. When you run NONMEM through PsN, you don't have to tell Pirana where NONMEM is located, since this is already specified in the `psn.conf` file of PsN.

3.2.1 Managing NONMEM installations

Existing NONMEM installations can be added to Pirana via the Settings menu, under the NONMEM tab. Here, both local (upper) and cluster (lower) installations can be added for use in Pirana. A *smart search* tool is implemented for local NONMEM installations, which searches for NONMEM installations in the most common locations on your local drives. If you have installed NONMEM in a non-common location, or want to use NONMEM on a remote cluster, add the paths to NONMEM manually.

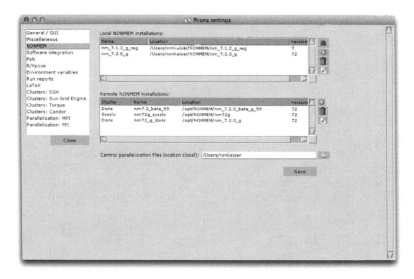

Figure 3.3: NONMEM settings window

3.2.2 Setting environment variables

NONMEM requires a Fortran compiler installed. For this compiler to function properly, it is important to set the environment variables correctly. Especially for Intel compilers, this can be trooublesome, as different environmental variables need to be defined. For GNU compilers, setting the PATH environment variable is usually sufficient. There are several ways you have control over the environment variables when using Pirana:

1. In the settings menu, under *Environmental variables*, the PATH variable used within the Pirana environment can be defined,

or additional folders can be added to the existing PATH. Also, additional environmental variables can be defined here.

2. Alerntatively, in the same settings screen for each nmfe-run that is started, you can specify a command that will be executed before starting nmfe-type runs, which can be e.g.

```
PATH=%PATH%;C:\gfortran\bin
```

3. At startup, Pirana will check for the existence of 2 files in the Pirana base folder: *set_env.txt* and *add_env.txt*. These files can be used to either set, or add to the system variables, respectively. The files may look e.g. like this:

```
PATH=C:\nmvi\run;C:\MinGW\bin
VARX=C:\bladibla;etc
```

3.2.3   Running models

As mentioned before, a model can be run using nmfe, *PsN* or *WFN* (WFN is Windows only). This can be done by selecting a model from the list, and right-clicking to show the context-menu. From here, you can either select nmfe, or the PsN or WFN options. The commands are also available from the toolbar. WFN is disabled by default.

Using nmfe

Execute a model using *Run (nmfe)*, or press Control-R. This will open up a dialog showing two additional options for running the model, e.g. which NONMEM installation to use, and if models should be executed in separate folders or on a cluster system.

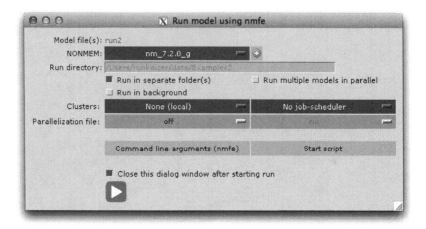

Figure 3.4: nmfe run window

Pirana supports the use of the parallelization functionality available in NONMEM 7.2+. When you select a NONMEM installation in the nmfe run window, the available parallization files (*parafiles*) are displayed under the parallelization tab. *Parafiles* can be generated using the Wizard in Pirana. You can also have Pirana generate the *parafile* on-the-fly (select *auto-MPI* or *auto-FPI*). Under Settings → Parallelization, the FPI and MPI files that Pirana generates can be specified.

Parallization files can be imported from local or remote locations. Local import can be performed through Settings → NONMEM. Remote parallelization files can be imported from a cluster location defined under Settings → SSH.

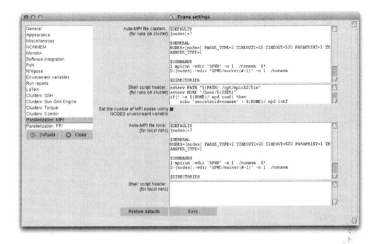

Figure 3.5: Automatic parallelization file

Using PsN

PsN is an extensive toolkit for advanced modeling & simulation, and contains essential tools such as bootstrapping, visual predictive checks (vpc), stepwise covariate modeling (scm), simulation and re-estimation (sse), and many more. All PsN-toolkit functions can be accessed from Pirana using the right-click menu or the toolbar. `execute` is also conveniently available using the *Ctrl-e* keyboard shortcut. The dialog window is then opened (shown below), which can also shows the PsN-help info for the selected command. By default, Pirana will show the dialog in *simple view*, while the *advanced view* will show more options e.g. for running R scripts before/after runs, and running on clusters and interacting with job schedulers. The command line editor can be used to specify additional parameters to the PsN funtion. Pirana stores each executed PsN command, which are available from the 'History' button.

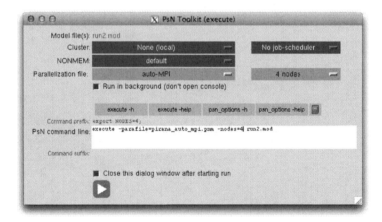

Figure 3.6: PsN dialog window

From the PsN tab in the Settings window you can define the default command line parameters for most PsN functions. Some of PsN's functions are not related to models, but to datasets, such as data_stats, *create_subsets* etc. These functions can be invoked from the file list on the right by selecting a file and opening the menu by right-clicking the mouse. A similar interface will be opened as for PsN's model functions.

Similar to the nmfe dialog window, the PsN dialog also offers the possibility to easily setup parallel execution. Pirana can be instructed to auto-generate the MPI/FPI file required for parallel execution. When MPI or FPI, and the number of nodes are selected, Pirana will automatically add the required PsN arguments (-parafile and -nodes).

Using Wings for NONMEM

On Windows, Pirana is capable of invoking the WFN-commands *nmgo* and *nmbs*, for run execution and bootstrapping respectively. Since WFN does not support multiple model files to be processed by its commands, when multiple models are selected, only the first model file is executed. When the WFN method is selected, two parameter specification bars will become visible. In the upper entry, run parameters can be specified, e.g. for the bootstrap: '1 100' to specify a bootstrap with 100 replicates. The lower parameter bar specifies command-line parameters used when starting WFN.bat, e.g. 'g77 std' for specifying the compiler and the NONMEM version to be used.

Note: What Pirana actually does when executing runs through WFN, is create a temporary batch-file in the current directory that starts *WFN.bat* to load the necessary environment variables, after which *nmgo* is started with the model-file and parameters specified.

28

3.3 Analyzing results & output

3.3.1 Main overview

After a model has been run/executed, and the folder is refreshed, Pirana will show the main results of the run in the main overview. It will show the OFV, the difference in OFV with the reference model (if specified), the number of significant digits, and some information about the estimation, i.e.:

S means a succesful minimization (as reported by NONMEM)

R means estimation ended with rounding errors

C means a succesful covariance step

M means an unsuccesful covariance step due to matrix singularity

B means a boundary problem was reported by NONMEM

Pirana can also show the AIC and BIC values for the model, although you will have to instruct Pirana explicitly to calculate them for finished runs. See 'Miscellaneous functionality' in this manual for more information.

3.3.2 Parameter estimates

A list of parameter estimates is shown in the right section of the Pirana window, if *Estimates* is selected as the active tab. It also shows the RSE for parameters (between round brackets), and shrinkage for the random effects (between square brackets). In this overview it is also highlighted if final gradients for a parameter were zero (red foreground), mean of eta-distribution was significantly different from zero (etabar, red background), boundaries were encountered (blue background), or parameters were fixed (grey background). A more detailed list is available by selecting *Models* → *Parameter estimates* from the right-click menu, or from the toolbar. If just one model is selected, Pirana will show all parameter estimates and associated RSE values, if available. If multiple models/runs are selected, Pirana will show the parameter estimates of these runs side by side, facilitating comparison. These results can be easily converted into csv, LATEX or HTML for e.g. reports or further analysis. The estimates can be exported by R as well, by clicking the R-icon in the parameter estimates area.

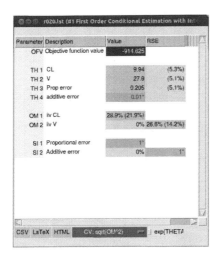

Figure 3.7: Parameter estimates window: Single run

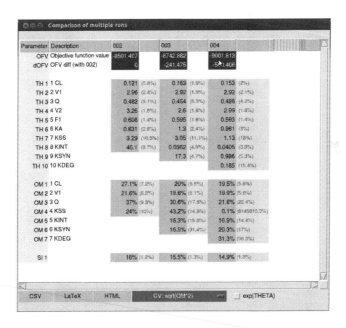

Figure 3.8: Parameter estimates window: Comparing multiple runs

3.3.3 Run Reports

Run reports with model and run info, and parameter estimates can automatically be generated, and outputted as HTML, LaTeX, Word, or plain text format. The reports optionally displays basic run information, run statistics, description and notes, and parameter estimations, split by implemented estimation methods. The information to be included in the report can be specified in the menu under *Settings* → *Run reports*. LaTeX output is opened in the specified code editor, but also can be converted automatically to PDF using pdflatex (if installed).

After a run report is generated it will show up in the list on the right, under the tab *Reports*. In this tab, also goodness of fit plots are shown, generated either using the Xpose GUI in Pirana, or the R scripts library. Double-clicking on any of the plots or reports will re-open them.

Note: In the run reports, Pirana calculates the RSE for population parameters as $RSE_{\theta_i} = \frac{SD_{cov,\theta}}{\theta_i}$, but doesn't take into account log-transformation of parameters (e.g. when MU-modeling). For inter-individual and residual variance (Ω and Σ), RSE's are calculated as e.g. $RSE_{\omega_{i,i}^2} = \frac{SD_{cov,\omega_{i,i}^2}}{\omega_{i,i}^2}$. RSE's given for $\omega_{i,i}$ and $\sigma_{i,i}$ are calculated as e.g. $RSE_{\omega_{i,i}} = \frac{SD_{cov,\omega_{i,i}^2}}{2 \cdot \omega_{i,i}^2}$

3.3.4 Intermediate results

When running models through any of the available methods (nmfe / PsN / WFN), the intermediate results (parameter estimates, objective function value, gradients) can be viewed by clicking on the *hourglass-icon* or from *Tools* → *Intermediate results*. This will open a window which shows the models that are currently running. By clicking on a run in the list, Pirana will parse the intermediate files and show the intermediate parameter estimates in the table and the plot. In the plot, you can choose to show either the gradients (if a gradient method is used), the intermediate estimates, or the objective function value (OFV). Make sure that you specify PRINT=1 and MSFO=xxxxx in the $ESTIMATION record, to be able to obtain regularly updated intermediate estimates. From the context menu, signals can be sent to currently running NONMEM processes, such as *stop* and *next iteration*.

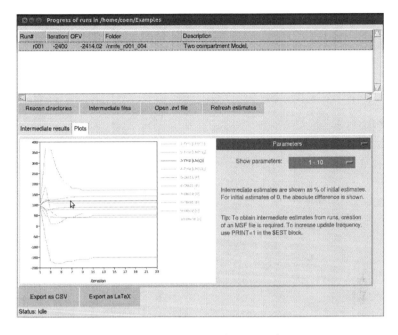

Figure 3.9: Intermediate results

3.3.5 Run Records

For all models in the current folder, or a selection thereof, a csv run record can be compiled by Pirana that includes all model and run characteristics, such as model description, estimation method, objective function value, termination result, etc. An abridged version of the run record can also be created as a plain text or Word document.

Visual Run Record

Pharmacometric model development most often progresses in a hierarchical fashion, using the likelihood ratio test to assess significance of improved fit between nested models. An appropriate visualization of the model hierarchy will help the modeler gain better understanding of key stages in model building, and willl aid in communicating the model development history to others. Such a visualization can be generated by Pirana, an example of which is shown below.

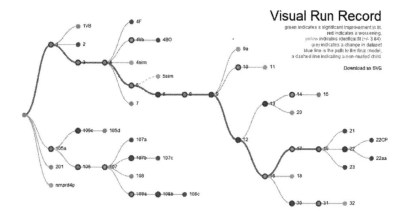

Figure 3.10: Visual Run Record

To create the VRR, Pirana produces Javascript code compatible with the Data-Driven Documents Javascript library (d3.js). The visualization can be generated as an SVG image in any modern internet browser. Several options are implemented that allow customization of the visualization, and both dynamic and static images can be created. In a VRR, the hierarchy of models is immediately visible, and using the dynamic collapsable dendrograms, non-relevant model threads can be hidden from the visualization. The VRR also shows additional model information when hovered over the nodes. Colors aid in visualizing the improvement / worsening of model fit (green / red), and whether the model has children or not. In each branch, the nodes are ordered by OFV. When a final model is specified, the modeling path can be made visible as a blue line, thereby easily identifying the key runs. The visualization can be implemented as a horizontal or radial tree, the latter of which can be used when the model tree is very large.

3.3.6 Data Inspector

Pirana is able to construct scatter plots using the built-in *DataInspector*, e.g. for quickly inspecting goodness-of-fit, covariate relationships, distribution of etas, performing data checkout etc. The DataInspector shows all the columns present in the dataset, which can be mapped to the X- or Y-axis (shown in figure 3.11). DataInspector can either be invoked by selecting a model (main overview), or a data file (from the list on the right). If a model is selected and DataInspector

is started, Pirana will gather the dataset specified in $INPUT and the
table files created in $TABLE. It will then ask the user which of these
files to open in DataInspector. If only one file is found, it will open
that one automatically.

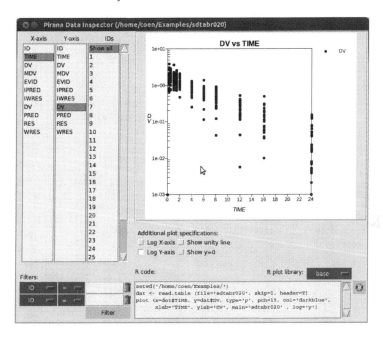

Figure 3.11: Pirana DataInspector

3.3.7 Visual run records

The model building process from initial to final model can be visual-
ized using the visual run record. This can be done via Results → Run
records → Visual run record. Here a final model can be selected, and
the visual run record will be graphically depicted.

Pirana can parse NONMEM-generated tables, and csv files. Multiple Y values can be plotted by holding the Control- or shift-key and
selecting multiple (up to three) data columns. Inside the plot, regions
of interest may be selected, which are then zoomed. Double-clicking
inside the plot region changes back to the previous view. Plots can be
filtered, which can be useful, e.g. to show only data for one patient,
or groups of patients or covariates.

In the text-box below the plot, code is generated that recreates the

34

same graph in R, either in *base, lattice,* or *ggplot2*. This code can be used as a starting point for the generation of plots for manuscripts or reports. Clicking the *R*-button will invoke the R-GUI or code editor.

3.3.8 R scripting for creating graphs and file processing

Pirana includes functionality to run custom R-scripts on output from models-executions such as NONMEM tables. Scripts can be written by the user, but a considerable collection of scripts is also bundled with Pirana, which can serve as starting point for your own implementations. Scripts are located in three locations, one for group-wide scripts (in the scripts-folder in the location where Pirana is installed), one for user-scripts (home/user/.pirana/scripts on Linux, C:\Documents and Settings\user\Application data\.pirana\Scripts on Windows), and one for project-specific scripts, stored in the sub-folder pirana_scripts in the current folder. The folder structure underlying the scripts folders is reconstructed within the scripts menu, and scripts can be edited either by editing them from outside Pirana, or by choosing them from the *Edit* menu option.

Scripts can be started by selecting a model, and selecting the desired script from the scripts menu located in tight tab panel. Pirana invokes R and runs the script in the directory pirana_temp underlying the active folder. However, before execution, Pirana replaces #PIRANA_IN with an R list-object which specifies model and results information, e.g. as:

```
models <- list (
   "003" = list (
      "modelfile"       = "003.mod",
      "description"     = "PK model digoxin",
      "reference_model" = "002",
      "data_file"       = "nm_pk_001.csv",
      "output_file"     = "003.lst",
      "tables"          = c("003.TAB", "sdtab003")
   )
)
```

To automatically load PDFs or images that are created by R after execution of the script, you should include e.g. the following line in the script:

```
#PIRANA model_output.pdf
```

35

where `model_output.pdf` is the file that you want Pirana to load. This may either be a PDF, or a common image format such as png, jpg, or gif. Please have a look at the scripts included with Pirana for examples this functionality.

Interactive scripts

Pirana also has the ability to create *interactive scripts*, meaning that upon execution of an R-script, the user will be presented with a dialog that asks for plotting and input options. The plotting options can be specified in the R-script like e.g.:

```
### <arguments>
###       <title label="Plot title">DV vs PRED</title>
###       <x_var label="X-variable">DV</x_var>
###       <xlab label="x-axis label">Dependent variable</xlab>
###       <y_var label="y-variable">PRED</y_var>
###       <ylab label="y-axis label">Pred. concentration</ylab>
###       <subset label="Subset string"></subset>
###       <split_id label="by ID" type="bool">FALSE</split_id>
### </arguments>
```

This will result in the following interface:

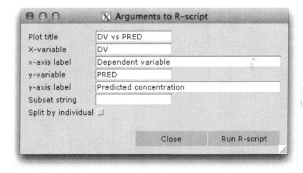

Figure 3.12: Interactive scripts

In the R-script, the specified options are then available as the list *arg*, e.g using:

```
ggplot (data=tab, aes (x=get(arg$x_var),
                    y=get(arg$y_var))) + geom_point()
```

3.3.9 Xpose support

After selecting a model, Xpose can be invoked from the scripts menu either by selecting the integrated Xpose GUI or the calling the (external) Xpose R-menu. The integrated Xpose GUI allows for execution of Xpose commands. The user can also add optional arguments to Xpose commands. Plots can be saved as PDF or PNG files, or Sweave/knitr code can be generated.

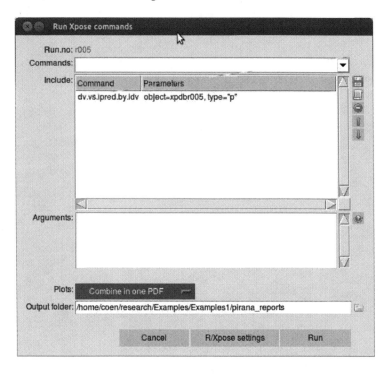

Figure 3.13: Xpose window

Besides the commands available in the list, you can also input your own commands or statements to the list. Lists can be saved for easy access later on. The general plotting arguments for pdf and png (e.g. width=10, height=8 can be set in the settings menu under *R/Xpose*)

3.3.10   Wizards

As mentioned earlier, Pirana comes with several wizards, such as a wizard to create a NONMEM model file, PsN-scm configuration files, and parallelization files. You can alter these Wizards to your liking, as they are implemented from wizard-specification files located in /wizards in the Pirana installation folder. Of course, it is possible to create your own Wizards as well. Just create a .pwiz file in the wizards-folder and follow the instructions in the template that is provided there. Wizards that are included with the current version of Pirana are described below:

PK model

This wizard allows stepwise construction of a range of PK models in NONMEM. It includes all ADVANs in NONMEM, all estimation methods, and the most commonly used residual error models. Of course, keep in mind that you have to change the initial estimates and the $DATA and $INPUT records to suit your PK problem.

NM parallelization file

NONMEM 7.2 and higher allow parallization of single runs, which requires a so-called parafile, a configuration file for the parallelization. These files can be created using this wizard.

SCM configuration file (PsN)

The scm command in PsN requires a configuration file. With this wizard you can create such a file, which includes the most commonly used options. Please note that more features are available in the scm tool than are offered as option in the Wizard, so it is advised to acquaint yourself with the full scm documentation.

Dataset template

This wizard can be used to create an R script that, in turn, generates a NONMEM simulation data file with specified number of individuals, doses, observations, dosing times, and covariates. This can be useful e.g. for quickly setting up simulations in NONMEM.

3.4 Model translation

Pirana can translate NM-TRAN models written in any ADVAN routine to ordinary differential equations (ODEs). The model can be exported to ADVAN6 (NM-TRAN), to R (using the deSolve library), Berkeley Madonna, MATLAB and PopED. Also several translators are included that translate specific parts of NONMEM code to alternate NONMEM code.

Translation to other tools

For R, a multidose simulation is automatically implemented, for the other converters only single dose simulation is implemented. Pirana currently does not read in the dataset to extract dosing information.

Pirana extracts the parameter estimates for the structural model (θ), and also the between subject variability matrix (Ω). The latter is however done only when simulating in R or Berkeley Madonna (not available for Matlab at current). No residual error model is currently implemented in any of the translators, but this can easily be added by the user.

Porting the model structure to PopED allows evaluation of optimal study designs (OD). Pirana creates the necessary files for PopED execution, however the user still needs to provider the details of the design and other optimization settings.

MU-model conversion

Pirana can convert standard NONMEM models to MU-model coding. At current, Pirana can only convert models written using normal- or log-normal ηs, e.g.

```
CL = THETA(1) * EXP(ETA(1))
```

will be converted into:

```
MU_1 = LOG(THETA(1)) ; ** MU-referenced by Pirana
CL = EXP(MU_1+ETA(1))
; Original equation: CL = THETA(1) * EXP(ETA(1))
```

Difference equations

For some models written in ODEs, writing some parts of the model in difference equations can considerably reduce computational burden, while maintaining parameter precision.[1] Pirana can help in setting this up: it will transport all code written in $DES other than the $\frac{dA}{dt}$ system to $PK, and adds some required code (using *MTIME*).

3.5   Batch operations

Pirana offers functionality to perform batch operations on a set of models, such as search and replace functions.

Search and replace in models Replaces a given search text with another string or block of text in the selected models.

Replace block This function enables you to replace a whole block of code in selected model files, e.g. the $DATA block if you want all model files to use a different data file, or the $THETA block if you want to use other initial estimates.

Add code to models With this function, lines of code can be added to the beginning or the end of selected models.

Add code to blocks With this function, lines of code can be added to a specific block in the selected models.

Batch duplicate Creates multiple duplicates of one model file, with (optionally) updated run/table numbers and final parameter estimates.

Random simulation seeds In all selected models, the $SIMULATION block will be updated with new seeds.

3.6   Miscellaneous functionality

NONMEM help files

Modeling with NONMEM, and construction of NM-TRAN syntax can be troublesome at times, and therefore it is convenient to have NONMEM's help files at your fingertips. Pirana provides a user interface to these help files, allowing you to filter on keyword. Before help file interface can be used, the NONMEM help files need to be imported as the files are not supplied with Pirana. For this, go to *Tools → NONMEM → Import / update NONMEM help files*. You can import

---

[1]Petersson KJ et al. J Pharmacokinet Pharmacodyn. 2010 Oct;37(5):493-506.

the information from a local NONMEM installation or from an installation located on a cluster (over SSH). After succesful import, the NONMEM help interface is availabe from the *Help* menu.

Code differences between models

Pirana provides a tool to show code differences, similar to the *diff* functionality on Unix systems. If one model is selected and the diff tool is activated (*Right-click menu → Model → Code difference between models*), Pirana will show the difference between that model and the reference mode (if specified). If two models are selected, Pirana will show the code differences between these two models.

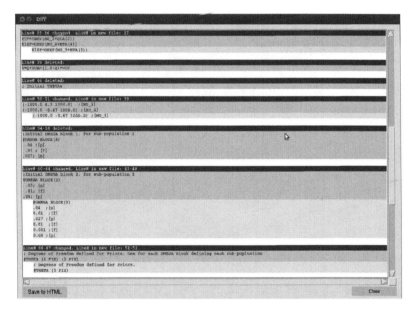

Figure 3.14: Code difference between models

Model Archive: Automatic backup of models and results

When editing and running models, Pirana can automatically backup all versions of controlstreams and result files. When this feature is activated (in the settings menu), intermediate versions of models and results are saved in a separate folder, every time a model is changed, or when a new results files is found. The archive can be accessed via the *Tools* menu, under the option *Model Archive*. Details of the run and (if applicable) parameter estimates can be reviewed. Also, different versions of models can be compared and restored. The internal Pirana database files (`pirana.dir`) are also backup up, if it has been more than a week since the previous backup.

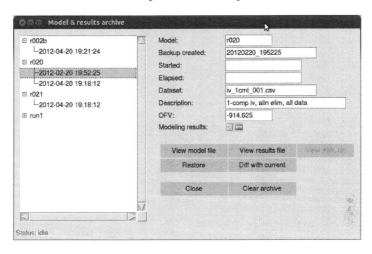

Figure 3.15: Model backup / archiving window

Matrices

Pirana can automatically extract the covariance, correlation and inverse covariance matrices from a NONMEM 7+ run (`cor/cov/coi` files), and show them in a spreadsheet-like window. These can then also be automatically exported to an R object, e.g. useful for simulation purposes.

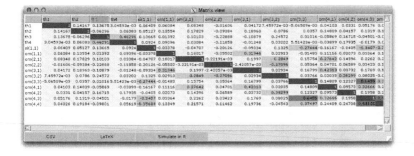

Figure 3.16: Correlation matrix

Miscellaneous tools

Correlation calculator This opens the built-in *Correlation Calculator*, which can be used to re-calculate a covariance to a correlation on the SD-scale. The formula for correlation that is used is:

$$\rho_{i,j} = \frac{\omega_{i,j}^2}{\omega_{i,i} \cdot \omega_{j,j}}$$

with ρ specifying the correlation between two elements (i,j) in a matrix, and ω specifying elements of Ω or Σ.

Checkout dataset This will create (and open) an HTML-file which displays a selected dataset using separate colors for different event-types. This will thus show the dataset in a slightly more convenient format for manual inspection than in a spreadsheet. The function needs at least the ID, TIME and EVID columns in the dataset to work properly.

Calculation of AIC/BIC Pirana can calculate the Akaike Information Criterion and the Bayesian Information Criterion. These criterions are defined as follows:

$$AIC = 2 \cdot k - 2 \cdot ln(L) \tag{3.1}$$

$$BIC = -2 \cdot ln(L) + k \cdot ln(n) \tag{3.2}$$

with k the number of parameters in the model, L the maximized value of the likelihood function, and n the number of observations in the dataset used in fitting the model. The calculation of these criterions is however not so straightforward for non-linear mixed-effects models, and the weights/penalties applied to parts of the equation can be different in different circumstances. Pirana allows the penalties to be changed when it calculates the AIC/BIC. From the right-click menu, select *Model actions → Calculate AIC/BIC*, and a dialog window will open which will present the options available. Some useful literature is listed below.

- Vaida and Blanchard, Conditional Akaike information for mixed-effects models. Biometrika, 2005. 92(2): p. 351-370.
- Liang, et al., A note on conditional aic for linear mixed-effects models. Biometrika, 2008. 95(3): p. 773-778.

- Hodges and Sargent, Counting degrees of freedom in hierarchical and other richly]parameterised models. Biometrika (2001) 88 (2): 367-379.

- Donohue et al., Conditional Akaike information under generalized linear and proportional hazards mixed models, Biometrika (2011) 98 (3): 685-700.

- Delattre et al., BIC selection procedures in mixed effcts models
http://hal.inria.fr/docs/00/69/64/35/PDF/RR-7948.pdf

Clean-up folder This tool can be used to clean-up files that NON-MEM generates when running a model (e.g INTER, FSTREAM, etc.). So if you run a model in the main model folder (which is not considered good modeling practice), you can use this tool to clean up after model execution.

3.7 Conventions and Methods

Model file conventions

- Users of PsN and Xpose likely follow the 'Uppsala convention' of having model files named like *run1.mod*, *run2.mod*, etc. This is recommended for Pirana users as well, although Pirana is flexible in this respect. Note that Pirana removes the run from the modelfile name in the model overview.

- Pirana looks for a description of the model in the first part of the model file. It adheres to PsN's run record standards. If the PsN run record is not used, Pirana searches for the words $PROBLEM or Model desc: to extract the model description.

- If you want to use the hierarchy functionality for models, you should specify the reference model in the first few lines of the model file. Again, best is to use PsN's run record specification, but Pirana is flexible and also compatible with Census, and understands the following syntaxes:

```
;; 1. Based on: 001.mod
; Ref. model:001.mod
; Ref:001.mod
; Parent=001.mod
```

- Model parameter descriptions need to be specified after a semicolon, e.g.

```
$THETA
(3, 5, 11) ; CL/F
(10, 50, 100) ; V/F
```

Note that Pirana reads these decriptions from the model file (and not from the output file). To be read correctly, covariance block need to be specified as:

```
$OMEGA BLOCK(2)
0.1 ; IIV CL/F
0.05 ; COV CL~V
0.1 ; IIV V/F
```

or as:

```
$OMEGA BLOCK(3)
0.1             ; IIV CL/F
```

45

```
0.05 0.1    ; IIV V/F
0.01 0.05 0.1 ; IIV KA
```

- When models are to be executed in a separate directory, files needed for compilation (e.g. additional Fortran routines in .FOR files), are copied automatically by Pirana. These files should be specified in the OTHER and CONTR entries on the $DATA record. If more additional files are needed, you can instruct Pirana to copy these by adding this line to your control stream:

```
; INCLUDE=file1_to_be_copied.ext,file2_to_be_copied.ext,
    etc
```

Note that PsN has it's own functionality for doing this.

3.8   Keyboard shortcuts

The following keyboard shortcurts are available in Pirana:

- Ctrl-R: Run model
- Ctrl-L: Open NM output file (.lst)
- Ctrl-N: New model file
- Ctrl-D: Duplicate model file
- Ctrl-P: Show parameter estimates for run(s)
- Ctrl-T: HTML-file from NM output
- Ctrl-E: Execute model (PsN)
- Ctrl-B: Bootstrap model (PsN)
- Ctrl-V: VPC from folder (PsN)
- Ctrl-U: Update inits (PsN)
- Ctrl-X: Run Xpose commands
- Ctrl-A: Select all models
- Ctrl-+/-: Increase / decrease font size
- Ctrl-, : Open settings window
- F5 : Refresh current folder

3.9 Command line parameters

- `-portable`
  Use Pirana in portable mode, e.g. from a USB-stick, leave no footprint on computer.
- `-console`
  Leave console window open. This may be useful when Pirana hangs or crashes, as sometimes an error may be shown on the command line. (Fortunately Pirana hardly ever crashes, though).
- `-debug`
  Print information during startup. This may be useful when for some reason Pirana doesn't start up, possibly due to some missing file or incomplete installation.
- `-dev`
  Pirana will show and allow use of experimental features (experimental features differ between versions).
- `-time`
  Print some information during folder reading. Useful for troubleshooting on slow network connections.

3.10 Troubleshooting / FAQ

Below are some answers to commonly asked questions. Note that a more elaborate and up-to-date FAQ is also available on the website.

- *Why the name Pirana?*

  An acronym for: Pirana is a Resourceful Assistant in NONMEM Analysis.

- I'm running on Windows, but for some reason Pirana won't start (anymore)

  Please check for any errors during startup by using the -console -debug arguments on the command line. If there is any problem during initialization of Pirana, you can try to reset the default settings in Pirana by running pirana.exe -refresh in the console (this works only in version 2.5.1 or later. For earlier versions, remove the folder %HOME%/.pirana manually, where %HOME% is your home folder). This will remove your current settings and re-install the defaults. Then, try to restart Pirana in the regular way. If this doesn't work, please report it as a bug with a screendump of the console output.

- *In Pirana's model overview table, I see some models but no results...?*

  First check if you have the extensions set correctly in preferences, e.g. .mod/.lst for model/results files. If this doesn't solve the problem, it may be due to the fact that your database file for that folder is corrupt. In the current folder, try renaming pirana.dir to pirana.dir.bak and refresh the folder. This error may sometimes occur when you have been using an old version of Pirana previously (<2.1.0). On Linux, problems have been reported with old versions of the Perl modules DBI and DBD::SQLite. Make sure you have versions 1.6 or higher or 1.14 or higher, of these respective modules. (You can check this by typing the following on the command line:

  ```
  perl -MDBI -e 'print "$DBI::VERSION"'
  perl -MDBD::SQLite -e 'print "$DBD::SQLite::VERSION"'
  ```

- *On startup of Pirana on Windows, it complains that it can't find the file* libgcc_s_dw2/1.dll, libstdc++-6.dll, *or* perl516.dll. Pirana needs these library files to function, and therefore we supply them with Pirana (in the folder where you installed it, probably C:\Program Files\Pirana). On some systems however, it needs to be copied to the folder "C:\Windows" or "C:\Windows\system3 for Pirana to function.

- *I can't seem to start any NONMEM runs or use PsN. Basically, noothing happens, and no error message is produced.*

  On Windows: The likely cause of this error is that Pirana can't start your command shell. Please check in your "Environment variables" in the Control panel, that

  ```
  C:\Windows\system32
  ```

  is included in the PATH environment variable. If not, add it. While you're at it, check also that the variable ComSpec is set to:

  ```
  C:\Windows\system32\cmd.exe
  ```

  on Mac OSX: This is most likely because Pirana is not able to find X-terminal. Please update your settings in Pirana, in *Settings → Miscellaneous → Terminal to start NONMEM runs in.* Change xterm into /usr/X11/bin/xterm, and it should work fine.

- *When I open a csv file in Excel from Pirana (and in general), I get the error message that the file is recognized as a SLYK-type file, and therefore cannot open the file.*

  This is due to the fact that the first column in your dataset is named ID. Renaming the column (e.g. id) or inserting a column before it will solve the problem. When converting and opening table files, the ID column is automatically converted to id by Pirana to avoid these issues.

- *Running on Mac OS X, after starting Pirana, nothing seems to happen.*

  Make sure you have Xcode, the Xcode command line tools, and XQuartz installed. Update to the latests OS X version.

- *Where does Pirana store the notes I make in the model overview?*

  Pirana stores your notes in a database-file (pirana.dir) in the current folder. So, if you would install a new version of Pirana, or move your model folder to another place, your notes will not be lost. The database file contains also some other information about the run results (OFV, run success, etc.) and can of course be read out manually as well, using `sqlite3`.

- *I'd like to cite Pirana in a report or article.*

  Please cite Pirana as: Keizer RJ et al.; Comput Methods Programs Biomed 2011 Jan;101(1):72-9; Piraña and PCluster: a modeling environment and cluster infrastructure for NONMEM. PubMed

3.11 Monolix

Since version 2.7.1, Pirana includes support for Monolix, the SAEM nonlinear mixed-effects modeling system developed by Lixoft. Pirana supports both the stand-alone version and the Matlab version of Monolix, and interacts with Monolix both on Windows and on Linux. Pirana requires that models are written in MLX-TRAN, the modeling language derived from NM-TRAN that can be used to write models in Monolix. Similar to NONMEM models, MLX-TRAN models are shown in the main overview automatically when a folder is loaded in Pirana. Pirana will automatically switch to *Monolix mode* when it detects MLX-TRAN models in the folder (the extension of which can be set under *Settings*). MLX-TRAN can be run from the Monolix submenu, and results and parameter estimates can be viewed in a similar fashion as the results obtained from NONMEM.

Note: The Monolix functionality in Pirana is still in development, and not all features available for NONMEM are available for Monolix. Also, a more detailed description of available features will be added to a future version of this manual. If you are interested to have Monolix-specific features implemented in Pirana, please let us know.

51

Chapter 4

Pirana and clusters

4.1 Clusters

Pirana supports interaction with Linux-based clusters on which NON-MEM and/or PsN are installed. The Job-schedulers Sun Grid Engine (SGE), Torque and Condor are supported. In addition, SSI-type cluster managers such as MOSIX should also work without problems. Connecting to a cluster is established using the SSH protocol, or any method that can be invoked from the command line. Two methods are available for using Pirana with a grid/cluster system, which involve installation of Pirana either on the local system or directly on the cluster server. The following paragraphs discuss these two separate methods.

Note: Single-system image clusters such as MOSIX, openMOSIX and Kerrighed distribute processes automatically accross nodes, and therefore no alternative setup is required in Pirana.

4.1.1 Method 1: Server-based installation

When using this approach, Pirana is only installed on the cluster-server, not on the local machine. Pirana is executed from the local machine using *X-over-SSH* window tunneling. This has the advantage of requiring only one central installation of Pirana for the entire modeling group, and Pirana and other modeling software is installed in a controllable environment. A disadvantage is that the interface is usually a bit slower. Also all auxiliary software (Office suite, HTML-browser, R and an R-GUI, etc.) resides on the cluster. Especially when using this method over larger distances (i.e. across internet), the performance of Pirana may be impaired due to the server-client transmission of the full GUI, but this of course depends on the bandwith of your connection and can be tested easily.

X-over-SSH tunneling

On the local machine it is necessary to have an X window system installed. For Linux users this is likely already installed. Mac OSX users need to install the XQuartz system. For Windows, a good X window manager is *Xming*, which can be obtained for free from `http://sourceforge.net/projects/xmi` After installation of Xming, start the Xming X-window server. An alternative to *Xming* is *Cygwin/X*.

Using the cluster

If everything is set up correctly, and the X-window server is started, Pirana on the cluster can be accessed through SSH, e.g. by using the SSH client. Now, you should be able to see the Pirana main window. If you get an error saying that the display cannot be started on localhost, you may have to enable X-window forwarding in OpenSSH or in PuTTY. When using PuTTY, it is essential to use the PuTTY terminal directly, and not plink.exe. The latter program tends to make Pirana crash often, probably due to terminal incompatibility. OpenSSH can also be used.

4.1.2 Method 2: Local installation

The other method is to install Pirana on the local machine, and connect to the cluster using Pirana and third-party SSH software. We usually recommended this installation approach as it offers a more stable interface (independent of network speed), and does not require installation of auxiliary software on the cluster. It will however require a few additional local installations. First, you need to mount the cluster drive with your data on your local PC (e.g. using sshfs on Linux/Mac or ExpanDrive on Windows). This can be set up e.g. using ExpanDrive to connect to the cluster through SFTP. Alternatively, if, on the remote cluster a Samba server is installed, a connection can be established by giving the following command:

```
NET USE Z: \ \server_name\<name> /user:<name> /persistent:yes
```

Both on Windows and Linux, you need to specify in the preferences the mounted remote diskspace and the local location, which is used by Pirana to translate local paths to paths on the remote cluster.
Secondly, an SSH client needs to be installed, which is probably already the case on Linux or Mac. On Windows, we have good experiences with PuTTY (http://www.chiark.greenend.org.uk/~sgtatham/putty/) and OpenSSH (download from http://sshwindows.sourceforge.net/).

In the *Settings → Clusters: SSH* menu, specify the command you use to connect to the cluster on the command line, e.g.:

```
ssh user@server.domain.ext
```

Note that Pirana needs passwordless SSH-access to the cluster, so make that you have an RSA key pair installed (explained in the next section). If you use PuTTY on Windows, you can also choose to supply the password on the command line instead, e.g.:

```
plink -l username -pw password server.domain.ext
```

although from a security perspective this is not recommended. Models can then be run in a similar fashion as explained in the section for running models locally, just select the cluster to run on from the nmfe- or PsN run windows.

Installing Public and private authentication keys

Either on Windows or Linux, type in a shell/console window: (If you use PuTTY instead of OpenSSH, use the Keypair generator program instead.)

```
ssh-keygen -t rsa
```

When asked for a passphrase, just press <Enter>. Now a public and a private key have been created in

```
c:\Documents and Settings\<Name>\.ssh}
```

(Windows) or

```
/home/username/.ssh
```

(Linux). In you home directory on the cluster, if it doesn't exist already, create the folder '.ssh'. In this folder, create the file 'authorized_keys' (no extension) and add the contents of id_rsa.pub to that file and save it. Now you should be able to login without being asked for a password. If SSH asks you if you want to accept the cluster as valid host, accept). Keep your private key secret. In the Pirana preferences, speficy the username to connect to the cluster (ssh_login).

Tip: if you experience delays (about 5 secs) when logging in to the server by SSH, this may be caused by a reverse DNS lookup. You can circumvent this by adding 'useDNS no' to the file /etc/ssh/sshd_config on the server. Restart the ssh server for the changes to take effect: sudo /etc/init.d/ssh restart

4.2   Interaction with job schedulers

Pirana has integrated support for Sun Grid Engine (SGE), Torque, and Condor job scheduling systems. In the settings menu, clusters and job schedulers can be configured. For Torque and Condor, auxilliary scripts can also be defined in the settings menu. Jobs submitted through SGE, Condor or Torque can be monitored and managed using the integrated job monitor (via View menu or top-right icon). If PsN is used, Pirana also indirectly supports the use of additional job scheduling systems that are supported by PsN (SLURM, LSF, UD, MOSIX, LSF). No integrated run managers are currently available in Pirana for these additional cluster systems.

4.2.1   Working with the SGE

Submitting the execution of a model using nmfe to the SGE, Torque, or Condor can be done by selecting the 'Run on SGE or Torque' from the *nmfe* or *PsN* dialog windows. This submits the model using *qsub* instead of starting it directly.

4.3   PCluster

Earlier versions of Pirana supported the construction of a simple Windows-based clustering system (PCluster). PCluster allows set up of a cluster using e.g. PCs of colleagues, and is easy to install on Windows systems. However, this kind of setup can nowadays be considered inferior to the clusters mentioned above in terms of stability and performance. The development of PCluster has therefore been discontinued, and no active support will be provided for this feature. If you still want to try the PCluster, there is a short legacy manual available upon request.

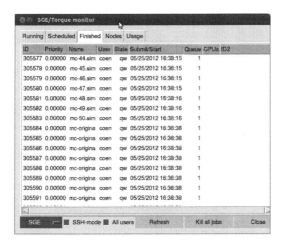

Figure 4.1: Job monitor

Chapter 5

Automated modeling workflow in Pirana

5.1 Background

An automated workflow alleviates the burden on modeling scientist by removing the repetitive task of running and evaluating many candidate models, standardizes the model development between modelers, and standardize the results reported from such an analysis ultimately leading to higher quality of PopPK analyses (*Schmidt et al. JPKPD 2014 Aug*). In Pirana (version >= 2.10), such a workflow is made available, and in this chapter we will walk through an example of an automated population PK analysis.

5.2 Tutorial

For this chapter, we will use the template model library that is provided with Pirana, and a (simulated) dataset of an iv-administered drug also provided with Pirana (demo.csv).

Start

In Pirana, create a new project folder somewhere on your hard-drive (or cluster). Browse into this folder (with Pirana). In this folder, copy the file demo.csv that is included in the Pirana installation folder

(Pirana/automod_library/demo/demo.csv). In Pirana, go to *Tools* →
Automated modeling workflow.

Screen 1: Models and dataset

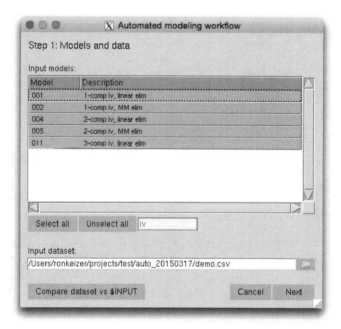

Figure 5.1: Screen 1: Models and dataset

This screen shows all models available in the library and which can
be selected to be included in the analysis. Use the filter for conveniently selecting e.g. only *iv* or only *oral* models. The dataset should
of course be specified as well before you can advance to the next step.
By default, it will use the first .csv file in this folder (in alphabetic
order).

When models and dataset have been selected, you should check whether
the $INPUT record in the models matches with the headers in the
dataset. For this, click the button *Compare dataset vs* $INPUT. This will
bring up screen shown in figure 2:

If the $INPUT in the models (shown in rows 2-...) does not match

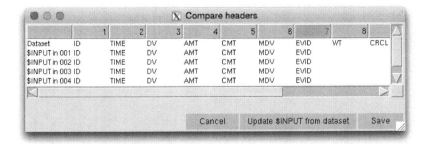

		1	2	3	4	5	6	7	8	
Dataset	ID	TIME	DV	AMT	CMT	MDV	EVID	WT	CRCL	
$INPUT in 001	ID	TIME	DV	AMT	CMT	MDV	EVID			
$INPUT in 002	ID	TIME	DV	AMT	CMT	MDV	EVID			
$INPUT in 003	ID	TIME	DV	AMT	CMT	MDV	EVID			
$INPUT in 004	ID	TIME	DV	AMT	CMT	MDV	EVID			

Cancel   Update $INPUT from dataset   Save

Figure 5.2: Compare/set input headers

up with the dataset (shown in row 1), you can click the button *Update $INPUT from dataset*. This will create a new $INPUT record for all models. After clicking *Save*, when the models will be written (in step 3 of the automated analysis), the $INPUT records in all models will be changed to the new one. It is left to the user to make sure that the variables used in the model are still included in $INPUT, as there is no extra check in place for that.

For our current analysis, we will select all *iv* models, so filter on *iv*, and select the remaining models. Update the $INPUT records, click *Save* and then *Next* to advance to the next step.

Screen 2: Setting initial parameter estimates

In the second screen, we can set initial parameter estimates, as well as lower and upper bounds. All parameters are read from the models that were selected in step 1. The parameter descriptions are defined in the models as comments to $THETA, $OMEGA, and $SIGMA blocks, like e.g.

```
$THETA
(0, 5, 100); CL
(0, 5, 100); V

$OMEGA
(0.1); CL
(0.1); V

$SIGMA
```

60

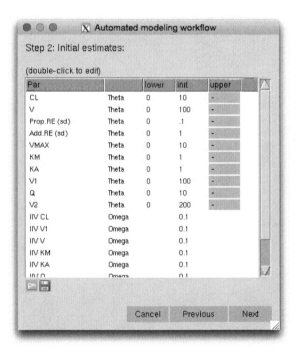

Figure 5.3: Screen 2: Initial parameter estimates

```
0.05 ; proportional error
```

Note: At current, correlations in $OMEGA and $SIGMA cannot be specified for an automated analysis. I.e. only the diagonal elements of $OMEGA and $SIGMA can be specified in the template models if you want to update them in this step. You can still include models that have full $OMEGA or $SIGMA blocks as template model, however you cannot provide descriptions (as comments) to the parameters in the block, and you cannot update them in this step of the analysis.

The two buttons below the parameter grid can be used to save and (re-)load parameter definitions to file.

For our analysis, let's leave the parameters as they are. Click **Next** to advance to the next step.

Screen 3: Folders

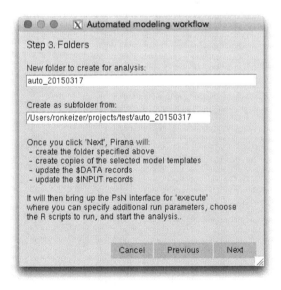

Figure 5.4: Screen 3: Folders

In this screen we can specify where to create the new models and run the analysis. By default it will generate a new folder name based on the current date, and as a subfolder from the current folder in Pirana. This screen also lists the actions that Pirana will perform once you click *Next*.

Let's use the defaults and click *Next*.

Screen 4: PsN dialog

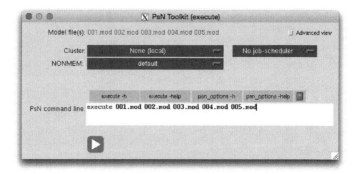

Figure 5.5: Screen 4: PsN

Pirana should now have switched automatically to the new folder where you will see the newly generated models. Pirana will also automatically bring up the PsN execute dialog. In this dialog, if you switch to *Advanced view*, you can select which R script(s) to run after all runs have been completed to generate goodness-of-fit plots. Click the *folder* icons next to the R scripts textboxes to select R scripts (or batch files) to run after (or before) the analysis (figure 6).

For our analysis, we will select the *Basic GOF plots as single doc* from the Reports folder to create GOF plots for all models. The graphical report will automatically be opened, but is also available from the *Reports* tab on the right.

If you have not selected R scripts to be executed automatically after the analysis has completed, you can still create them afterwards by selecting the runs and running any R script from the *R* tab on the right side of the Pirana window.

Besides the graphical report, Pirana can generate a *numeric* report for

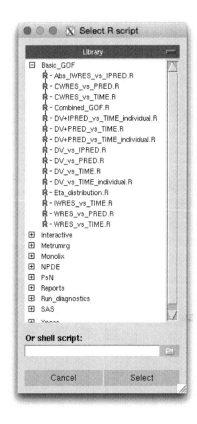

Figure 5.6: Select R script

the analysis, including e.g. OFVs, basic run information and parameter estimates. This document is not generated automatically but has to be requested manually after the analysis is complete: Make sure Pirana is still in the folder where the analysis was run, and then go to *Tools → Automated modeling workflow → Report*. On the first page you will see an overview of all models included in the analysis and their respective OFV, AIC and BIC (figure 7). The subsequent pages includes information on each individual run in the analysis.

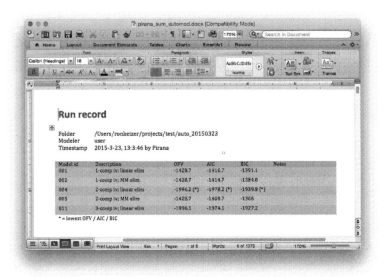

Figure 5.7: Report in Word

Chapter 6

cPirana

cPirana is a simple, *lite* version of Pirana that runs on the Unix command line. There are several reasons that we think cPirana is a useful addition to our primary software product: many –usually more experienced– modelers prefer to work from the command line. However, it is our opinion that a user interface (be it graphical or console-based) can greatly increase productivity and make the modeling process easier in general. For those modelers, we hope cPirana is a welcome addition to their workflow.

Secondly, while working on cluster through a slow internet connection, the interface of the Desktop version may become slow. Version 2.7.0 of Pirana included many speed improvements that improves working on slow connections. However, e.g. when traveling, one might be only interested in making a few small code changes and restart a model. For such use-cases, we consider cPirana to be a useful tool.

Finally, already from our earliest versions of Pirana, we intended to extend the implementation of Pirana to smartphone or tablets, allowing for increased mobility and connectivity. cPirana actually offers this possibility: if cPirana is installed on the Linux cluster that runs NONMEM and PsN, the user can connect from a tablet or smartphone using specialized ssh-apps (such as 'Prompt' on the iPad), to connect.

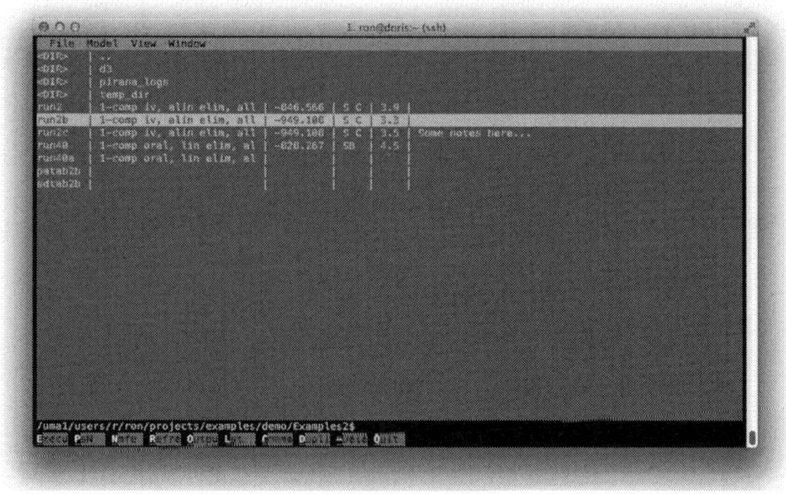

Figure 6.1: cPirana interface example

6.1 Installing cPirana

6.1.1 Using cPirana

Copy the contents of the linux installation zip-file file to a location on your system. Pirana is started using the command (assuming you installed it in the folder /pirana inside your home folder):

```
perl ~/pirana/cpirana.pl
```

cPirana will use the current folder as it's working folder. To make cPirana more easily accessible, add it as an alias to your .bashrc file, e.g.

```
alias cpirana="perl ~/pirana/cpirana.pl"
```

Now you can browse to any folder, and start the program from there using the cpirana command.

Chapter 7

Validation

Of course, the information gained from NONMEM or auxiliary tools must be reliable and accurate. Validation of these tools is therefore an important consideration. The main aim of Pirana is to provide overviews of modeling results and providing interfaces to other software (NONMEM, PsN, R, Xpose). As such, Pirana does not perform many calculations of its own. However, Pirana does perform some data parsing, formatting and reporting, i.e. when creating run reports etc.

The Pirana development team has developed tools that perform a validation of parts of this ecosystem. At current, we have two tools available:

psn-validate is a command-line tool that performs a series of pre-specified numerical tests, based on output from PsN tools. In the comparisons, the output from the specific PsN version that is to be validated (*test*-output) is compared to previously obtained output from a PsN version that is trusted, or has been validated in other ways (*reference*-output). The tools is scriptable, and includes R-scripts to perform the numerical comparison. It is however completely flexible, i.e. it allows custom R-scripts to be provided to perform the tests. The tool is available here: `https://github.com/ronkeizer/psn-validate`. Note: recently, the developers of PsN also released their own PsN validation suite with similar functionality.

pirana-validate is a command-line tool that perform a series of numerical test on the parameter estimates outputted by Pirana.

The parameters (*test*) are compared to those extracted by PsN's sumo tool (*reference*), for a user-specified library of models and modeling result files. This tool therefore solely focuses on Pirana and PsN's algorithms extraction of parameter estimates from NONMEM output files. Ultimately, this is Pirana's key feature, since Pirana does not perform many calculations, but is primarily a tool to generate overviews of results and allow the modeler to interpret results easier. The tool is currently not publicly available from the Pirana website but can be supplied upon request.

IMPORTANT: We do not claim any responsibility for the outcome or validity of the validation analyeses obtained using these tools. For example, we cannot guarantee that regulatory autharities accept particular validations performed with these tools, nor do we claim the correctness of the validation results. Please align intended validation procedure with the relevant authorities and internal QA/QC procedures.

7.1 Pirana validation tool

While a few models and model outputs are supplied with the Pirana validation tool, it is expected that the user provides a library of models and NONMEM output files (usually .lst or .res files) as reference. The Pirana validation tool expects a specific directory structure:

```
\val_library
   - \res1
       - \model
   - \res2
   - \res3
```

The valpirana Perl script is invoked from the command line, using e.g.:

```
perl validate.pl -ini=val_pirana20130224.ini
```

pirana-validate will then read the ini-file, and loop (alphabetically) through all folders in the folder specified in the ini-file. In each folder, it will extract all parameter estimates and standard error estimates (if available) using Pirana's internal NONMEM output parsing routines. It will then run PsN's sumo command, and store the parameters outputted by PsN to memory as well. These will then be compared, allowing for a pre-specified tolerance due to rounding. The ini-file should be specified similar to:

```
[general]
mod=mod
lst=lst
psn_dir=/usr/bin/
pirana_modules=/shared/val/pirana_modules_270
tol=

[lib1]
folder=/shared/val/valpirana_

[lib2] # Optionally, specify multiple libraries
folder=
```

Pirana pre-release validation

Before every Pirana release from version 2.4.0 upwards we used (predecessors of) the pirana-validate tool to check that the parameter estimates that Pirana extracts from NONMEM output files match those reported by PsN's sumo command. For this purpose, we've gathered more than 50 model and results files from multiple modeling groups and many different modelers. While we cannot share the model and output in the validation library, if you would like a report of the validation procedure for a specific version, please contact us.

7.2 PsN validation tool

The PsN validation tool compares output from a *test*-installation of PsN, with output from a trusted (previous) PsN installation. Tests can be implemented for any of the tools in PsN (e.g. execute, bootstrap, vpc, etc), and multiple tests can be performed for each tool (recommended). The tests to be performed are specified in a setup file. Customizable R scripts are used to perform the actual validation step for the tool. Every validation run is started by invoking the valpsn command:

```
./valpsn ex1\_20130201.ini
```

This bash script invokes the main perl script that acutally performs the validation. The script will read in the configuration file, and will perform all the specified validation elements in the sequence specified in the configuration file. The specific tests in the validation run are all implemented in R scripts, and should output SUCCESS or FAILURE. For every PsN tool a test script is provided with the tool, but the user is encouraged to write custom scripts. More info is available in the specific manual for this tool (available upon request).

Chapter 8

Endnotes

8.1 Acknowledgements

Many Pirana users are recognized for their valuable suggestions and bug-reports, especially those in the Uppsala, Amsterdam, and Cape Town pharmacometrics groups.

8.2 Bug reporting / suggestions

If you find any bugs, please report them at the support section of our website (http://www.pirana-software.com). A ticket will be created, and we will get back to you as soon as possible. Please be as specific as you can about the issue and report version number, system characteristics, and if relevant provide screenshots and model/results files. Requests for further improvement of Pirana are very welcome as well and can also be reported at the support section.

Part II

Tutorial: Pirana, PsN & Xpose

Chapter 9

Tutorial

The tutorial presented here is a tutorial on the use of PsN, Xpose, and Pirana combined, and has been published before (*Modeling & simulation workbench for NONMEM: tutorial on Pirana, PsN and Xpose; Keizer RJ, Karlsson MO, Hooker AC,* CPT-PSP 2013). The tutorial provides an excellent introduction to Pirana's basic functionality, and its connections to the other tools. This tutorial is aimed at modelers that have some familiarity with NONMEM, but have no or limited experience with PsN or Xpose. The training material and solutions are available from the Pirana website, or from CPT-PSP.

9.1 Introduction

Several software tools are available that facilitate the use of the NON-MEM software and extend its functionality. This tutorial shows how three commonly used and freely available tools, Pirana, PsN, and Xpose, form a tightly integrated workbench for modeling & simulation with NONMEM. During the tutorial, we provide some guidance on what diagnostics we consider most useful in PK model development, and how to construct them using these tools.

9.2 Background

Started in the early 80s with the development of the NONMEM (acronym based on NON-linear Mixed-Effects Modeling) software[1], population analysis has proven to be extremely useful within pharmacometrics, both in the development of new drugs[2] and the improvement of therapy with approved drugs.[3] Development of the NONMEM software continues, and, although over time several other modeling software tools have become available, NONMEM is still regarded as the gold standard within the pharmacometric community: a recent survey identified NONMEM (together with PsN[4]) as the most frequently used software tool by far.[5] Modeling and simulation in clinical pharmacology, and the use of NONMEM in particular, however, has a steep learning curve for most starting researchers. This is partially due to the fact that NONMEM is invoked from the command line, and models are implemented using a Fortran-derived syntax (NM-TRAN). Additionally, at its core, NONMEM performs only model estimation (or simulation), and the implementation of essential diagnostic tools such as bootstrap analyses and the creation of goodness-of-fit plots are left to the modeler. Therefore, alongside the development of NONMEM, many third-party tools have been developed that facilitate the use of NONMEM by providing tools for organization and automation. In this tutorial we will demonstrate the use of some of the most widely used auxiliary software tools: PsN, Xpose[6], and Pirana[7]. All three tools are released under an open source license and are freely available (except for the commercial use of Pirana, for which a commercial license is required). Separately, each tool offers useful functionalities, but there is a synergistic benefit as well when used together.

The aim of this tutorial is to show how these three tools provide a comprehensive workbench for modeling and simulation. This will be done by showing examples of the most often encountered steps in PK model development, i.e. a covariate modeling procedure and model evaluation using residual- and simulation-based diagnostics. However, the aim of the tutorial is not to provide guidance on how to perform a population PK analysis, but strictly on these software tools. A detailed overview of important aspects in population PK analyses has recently been presented in this journal, and we refer the reader to that article for guidance.[8] The current tutorial is structured in three parts: first a brief introduction to these software tools is given, explaining their basic purpose. In the main part of the tutorial, we show how a typical PK model building analysis is performed with these tools and NONMEM. At the end of the tutorial, several interesting additional features are highlighted for each specific tool. We will assume the reader is already somewhat familiar with NONMEM, although we have made efforts to present and discuss the tools in a general fashion where possible. All of the presented models, datasets, output, and diagnostic plots are available in the online materials.

Software

In this tutorial we will use NONMEM 7.2, Pirana 2.7.0, PsN 3.5.3, and Xpose 4.3.5. It is likely that future versions will behave similarly, but in earlier versions not all functions presented here may be available. We will show screenshots taken from Windows, but all programs discussed here function similarly on all major operating systems.

NONMEM [9] is modeling software that allows the user to estimate parameters in mixed-effects models (population approach) based on maximum likelihood- or Bayesian techniques that use either gradient or stochastic estimation methods. NONMEM translates model code written in a unique Fortran-based syntax (NM-TRAN) into pure Fortran code, which is then compiled and executed. NONMEM is currently developed by ICON Development Solutions under a proprietary software license.

PsN [4] is a combination of tools for performing advanced modeling & simulation (M&S) with NONMEM. It allows the implementation of bootstraps, visual predictive checks and many other useful functionality. PsN is written in Perl (and needs Perl installed, freely available for all major operating systems), and is operated from the command-line. Development started in 2000, and updates have been released with regular intervals.

Xpose [6] is a tool for plotting and analyzing NONMEM output, developed as a module for the R software (http://cran.r-project.org/, open source, S-based statistical software). The tools in Xpose can be used from the R command line or from a text-based menu system in R. Xpose was first released in 1998, and was initially developed for S-Plus. The current version (main version number 4) is however released exclusively for R and builds upon the lattice module for plotting. Both PsN and Xpose are developed at Uppsala University and are released under an open-source license (GNU v2).

Pirana [7] is a graphical user interface for NONMEM, PsN and Xpose/R. It has functionality for model management, model execution, output generation, interpretation of results, and includes many

other tools. Development of Pirana started in 2007 at the Nether-
lands Cancer Institute / Slotervaart Hospital (Amsterdam, NL),
and is currently continued by Pirana Software & Consulting BV
(http://www.pirana-software.com). Pirana is released under
an open source license (Creative Commons) for academic users
as well as a commercial license.

9.3   Tutorial

In this tutorial, file and folder names are shown in *italic*, Pirana actions are shown *red-italic*, while commands, arguments, NONMEM
syntax and screen output are shown in `fixed-width font`. We will
step through an example model building exercise, with the intent of
showing how to create, manage, and evaluate pharmacokinetic (PK)
models for a given dataset. The PK dataset used in this tutorial (*pk-
tab1*) is available in the on-line material, and contains plasma con-
centration data obtained from a simulated clinical trial of a novel iv
drug, performed in 50 patients, measured at 8 time points. All model
files that are mentioned in this article are also available on-line and
can be used as reference. Make sure that all software is installed correctly, and NONMEM runs can be started from both PsN and Pirana
(visit the respective websites for installation instructions), and that
the Xpose4 package is installed in R. Create a folder for this analysis
somewhere on your hard-drive, and put *pktab1* in this folder. Browse
to this folder in Pirana, and save it as the project TutorialPSP (*button
4 in figure 1*). As starting point for NONMEM models, it is often easiest to use the PK model wizard in Pirana, or start from one of the
models available in the model library. Start the wizard dialog window in Pirana (*Tools → Wizards*) and choose the PK model wizard,
and explore the options. However, for this tutorial we have already
provided the first model (run1.mod): copy the model run1.mod from
the online material to the folder you created. This model should now
be visible in the Pirana main model list when you direct Pirana to the
right folder (if not, refresh *Pirana button 5 in figure 1*).

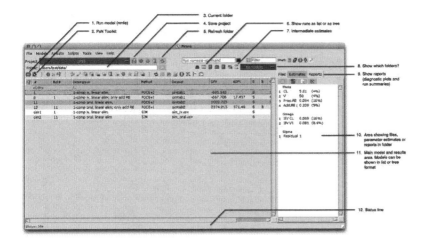

Figure 9.1: Pirana main screen

If you run from a model created by the wizard, make sure that the columns in the dataset match up exactly with the records specified in the $INPUT record in the model file. For the provided run1.mod this has already been done.

First runs

If we would invoke the native NONMEM run script, we would run e.g.

```
nmfe72 run1.mod run1.lst
```

but Pirana automates this in a dialog window: (*select model → right click → NONMEM → nmfe*). Several options are available to configure how and where (local or on a cluster) to run the model, or whether to submit it to a job scheduler. If you choose to run your models in Pirana through nmfe, you need to configure a NONMEM installation in Pirana (*Settings → NONMEM*). Select the quick-find option to scan your hard-drive for common installation locations for NONMEM. If NONMEM is not found there yet, specify the location yourself.

In this tutorial we will however not use nmfe, but only PsN to run models. There are multiple benefits of using PsNs execute over the regular nmfe command, the main ones being that models are run in separate folders, runs can be restarted automatically upon crashes and unsuccessful minimizations, and initial estimates can be tweaked.

Select the model and *right click* → *PsN* → *execute*. Pirana will show a similar dialog window as shown for nmfe, but now the command line for PsNs execute tool is shown (figure 2). For our first run, we will use the default command:

```
execute run1.mod
```

After clicking the run button, if PsN and Pirana are set up correctly, a console window will open with the following message:

```
Starting 1 NONMEM executions. 1
in parallel.
S:1 ..
```

which indicates that one model estimation has been started. The actual NONMEM process will run in a subfolder created by PsN. By default this will be */modelfit_dir1*, but a custom folder name can be specified using the -dir argument. If the argument -model_dir_nameis specified, PsN will automaticlly choose an informative foldername, in this case */run1.mod.dir.1*.

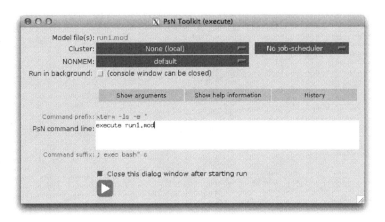

Figure 9.2: PsN dialog window

Check that inside the folder created by PsN, a subfolder is created in which the NONMEM process actually runs (*/NM_run1*). In Pirana, PsN folders are hidden by default, as they may quickly clutter the model overview. To unhide them again, select either PsN folders or All folders from the folder selector (button 7 in figure 1). Many additional arguments can be supplied to PsN commands to customize how PsN runs the NONMEM model, e.g.:

```
execute run1.mod -dir=test1 retries=3 -parafile=mpi6.pnm
   nm_version =nm72
```

which will run model run1.mod in the folder /test1. PsN is also instructed now to run using NONMEM version 7.2, parallelized using MPI (specified in configuration file mpi6.pnm), and to retry three times if the model doesnt converge in the initial run, each time changing the initial estimates of the parameters. A list of all available arguments including help information is available from the PsN dialog window in Pirana (figure 2), which is similar to using the -h and help arguments on the command line. In the PsN configuration file (*psn.conf*), a list of default arguments can be supplied as well, so commonly used arguments do not have to be repeated on the command line.

Results evaluation

After estimation has completed, refresh the Pirana main overview again. Basic results are now shown for the run, such as the objective function value (OFV), whether minimization was successful (S), and whether the covariance step was successful (C). If the run was successful, PsN will automatically copy back the results file (*run1.lst*) and the produced output tables (sdtab1, patab1) to the parent folder, which are then parsed by Pirana upon refreshing. Select the model again, and now select the *Estimates tab* from the right section of the Pirana window (11 in figure 1). The right section will then show the parameter estimates for this run. A more detailed overview that will e.g. show full random effect blocks can be opened from here. Create a run summary in Word format (alternatives are HTML, plain text or LaTeX), from the *menu → Results → Run Reports → Word*.

Diagnostic plots are a main decision tool in pharmacometric model development, in which a distinction can be made between residual-based diagnostics (goodness of fit plots based e.g. on residuals plotted versus time or model predictions), and simulation-based diagnostics (e.g. visual predictive checks, VPC). Obviously no strict rule should be applied here, but in our experience residual-based diagnostics are more useful in the first stages of model development, while simulation-based diagnostics are more useful in the latter stages of model development. Depending on what part of the model is diagnosed, different diagnostic plots will be useful, and most likely no single plot will suffice to evaluate model fit. Suggestions for diagnostic plots for specific model parts are shown in table 1. Note that this list is not exhaustive, and in addition, more specific plots may be required for appropriate diagnosis.

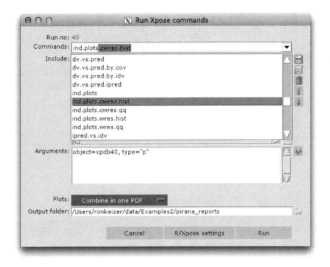

Figure 9.3: Xpose dialog window

For the current analysis, we will first have a look at some basic, residual-based goodness of fit plots. A general model diagnostic is the plot of weighted residuals versus time, or versus model predictions. For models run with the conditional estimation method (FOCE), it is most appropriate to use conditional weighted residuals (CWRES, [10]).

Table 9.1: Suggested diagnostic plots in Xpose for PK development

Model	Diagnostic plots
Residual error model	• Individual weighted residuals versus individual predictions (absval.iwres.vs.ipred) • Distribution / qq-plot of IWRES (iwres.dist.hist/qq) • In case of shrinkage: CWRES (cwres.dist.hist) or IWRESnpde • Autocorrelation in residuals (autocorr.iwres)
Between subject variability model	• Distribution / qq-plot of EBEs (parm.hist.hist/qq) • In case of shrinkage: distribution of EBE_{npde} • Correlation between parameters (parm.splom)
Inter-occasion variability model	• EBE parameter values vs occasions • Distribution / qq-plot of EBE (parm.dist.hist/qq) • In case of shrinkage: distribution of EBE_{npde}
Absorption model]	• Individual profiles (ind.plots) • CWRES vs time after dose (cwres.vs.tad) • Individual g.o.f. plots (dv.vs.pred.ipred.by.idv) • Distribution of absorption parameters (ka, MTT, F) (parm.hist)

Disposition model

- Residuals versus time (cwres.vs.idv)
- Individual profiles (ind.plots)
- VPC (xpose.VPC)

Covariates

- Parameter (EBE) vs covariate (parm.vs.cov)
- In case of shrinkage: EBEnpde vs covariate
- G.o.f. plots by covariate (dv.pred.vs.idv.by.cov)
- Correlations between covariates (cov.splom)
- Influential individuals (dOFV.vs.id)
- VPC stratified by covariate (xpose.VPC)
- VPC with covariate as IDV (xpose.VPC)

Use the Xpose GUI within Pirana to create these plots: *select model → right click → Xpose → Xpose GUI*. Add the plot `cwres.vs.pred` and `cwres.vs.idv` to the list of plots, and possibly some additional goodness-of-fit plots (a list of useful Xpose plots is given in table 2). In these plots you should observe an obvious pattern in the residuals. It may not be obvious immediately what is the cause of the misspecification, but a look at the individual plots (`ind.plots`) probably gives more insight: the model seems to be missing the bi-phasic nature of the observed data. Therefore, in the next step we will add distribution of drug into a peripheral compartment to our PK model, but first we will briefly discuss how to keep track of model development

Besides the Xpose GUI, there are several alternative ways of creating diagnostic plots from Pirana:

- DataInspector: a quick and flexible method for creating diagnostic plots based on NONMEM output, or checking input datasets. Select the DataInspector for *run1.mod* (*right click → Model → Open DataInspector*). Pirana will ask you now which input- or ouput file to open, choose the file sdtab1. In the DataInspector window, the variables on the x- and y-axis can be easily changed to any variable in the dataset, and filters can be applied on patient ID, or on any other variable. From this window, R-code can be generated that will recreate the same graph in R.

- R script library: Pirana comes bundled with a library of diagnostic R scripts, which can be run automatically from Pirana. Select a model and select the one of the R-scripts from the Scripts Tab, e.g. *Basic GOF → DV vs IPRED*, and then select Run script from the buttons above the list. The requested plot will be created in a PDF document and opened. Created plots will be listed in the Reports tab (10 in figure 1). The standard scripts bundled with Pirana can be extended and customized easily, but that is beyond the scope of this tutorial. Please refer to the manual and default scripts for guidance.

- Xpose menu system in R: The Xpose menu system can be started from Pirana (*right click → Xpose → Start Xpose menu in R*), or manually from an R session by invoking:

```
library(xpose4)
xpose4()
```

Xpose will then ask for the run number, which is used to determine which tables to import. Note that to use Xpose, NONMEM needs to be instructed to output tables that adhere to a specific naming and structure (see online materials table I, or the Xpose website). If you didnt use the Pirana model wizard to create the tables, add them manually in the NONMEM model file, using e.g.:

```
$TABLE ID TIME IPRED IWRES EVID MDV
       NOPRINT ONEHEADER FILE=sdtab1
```

From the Xpose menu system, goodness-of-fit plots can be created, e.g. browse to

```
4: Goodness of fit plots
2: Basic goodness of fit plots
```

Table 9.2: Commonly used arguments for Xpose functions

Function	Description	Commonly used arguments
basic.gof	Compound plot of basic goodness-of-fit plots	use.log, force.wres
y-var.vs.x-var	General diagnostics functions: y-var can be one of dv, pred, ipred, iwres, cwres, wres. x-var can be any of pred, ipred, idv. Add .by.cov or .by.idv to the command to split the plot by covariate or by individual.	abline, smooth
ind.plots	Plots of dv, pred and ipred versus time, split by individual.	y.vals, layout
xpose.VPC	Visual predictive check (uses PsN output folder)	VPC.info, VPCtab, PI.ci, PI.real, type
xpose.VPC.categorical	Visual predictive check for categorical data	level.to.plot, max.plots.per.page
xpose.VPC.both	Visual predictive check for continuous and categorical data (e.g. BLOQ data)	See above
autocorr.cwres	Plot cwrest+1 vs cwrest to check for autocorrelation in residuals	type, smooth, ids
parm.hist / parm.qq	Plot distributions / qq-plots of model parameters	onlyfirst
parm.vs.parm	Plot model parameter versus model parameters	onlyfirst, abline, smooth
parm.vs.cov	Plot parameters and etas versus covariates to check for correlation	onlyfirst, smooth
xpose.gam	Generalized Additive Models (covariate model building tool)	parnam, covnams, start.mod
basic.model.comp	Compare basic goodness-of-fit plots between two models	object.ref
kaplan.plot	Visualizes data and VPC from survival models	x, y, id, data, by

For most functions listed above, the following general arguments are useful: object (which Xpose database to use), main (plot title), inclZeroWRES (include values where WRES is zero).
In R, help information for functions can be obtained by giving the command ?¡function¿ where ¡function¿ is the desired R/Xpose function.
Abbreviations: dv = dependent variable, idv = independent variable, (c/i)wres: (conditionally / individual) weighted residuals. pred = population predictions, ipred = individual predictions.

Model management in Pirana

In M&S projects in both academia and industry, it is essential to keep track of the model development history. Pirana and PsN offer a tool to aid the modeler with this through the run record. The run record entails a standardized way of keeping track of model meta information such as the parent model, a description and/or a label for the model, and other information about the model components. We consider it good modeling practice to create a new model file for every change that is made to a model.

Duplicate the first model in Pirana (*right click on run1.mod → File actions → duplicate*). In the dialog that will open up, *run2.mod* is suggested as new model file name, and we can select which model is the reference model for this model (*run1.mod*), and optionally update the initial estimates with the parameter estimates from the reference model. The model description and other meta-information is stored in the model file itself using the run record syntax (also see the userguide for the run record on the PsN website). Pirana can show the main model overview as a list or as a tree (button 6 in fig 1), and can export a copy of the run record to various formats including comma separated (*csv*) files, HTML files and Word documents (*Results → Run records*), or create an interactive visualization of the model development tree or visual run record[11] like shown in figure 4 (*Results → Run records → Visual run record*).

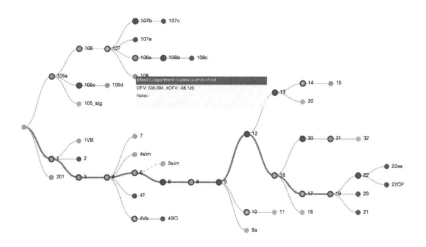

Figure 9.4: Visual Run Record

After duplication, the model *run2.mod* will be shown in the model overview, and opened in the editor, where we will now add a peripheral compartment to the model error model: change $SUBROUTINE to use ADVAN3 and TRANS4, change the parameter V into V1, and add to $PK:

```
Q = THETA(3)
V2 = THETA(4)
```

Of course, initial estimates for the intercompartmental distribution (Q) and peripheral compartment (V2) have to be specified as well in $THETA. For now we chose to run this model without IIV on these parameters. Run this model using execute, evaluate the drop in objective function, and compare the diagnostic plots for run2 to those made for run1. You should encounter a considerable drop in the objective function value, and find that the diagnostic residual plots show much improved model fit.

Next, we will diagnose the residual error model, for which an important diagnostic plot is that of absolute individual weighted residuals (|IWRES|) versus individual predictions (IPRED). For a true model, the distribution of absolute residuals should be similar over the whole range of the x-axis variable. If a homoscedastic error structure (additive error) was implemented in *run1.mod* and *run2.mod*, the plot will show larger residuals at higher individual predictions. This should therefore lead you to conclude that a heteroscedastic (combined proportional and additive) error model should provide a better description of the data. Therefore, create a new model (run3.mod) based on run2.mod and implement a combined error model using e.g.:

```
Y = IPRED * (1+EPS(1)) + EPS(2)
W = SQRT(IPRED**2*SIGMA(1,1)**2 + SIGMA(2,2)**2)
IWRES = (DV-IPRED)/W
```

It must be noted that the plot mentioned above is only informative at low -shrinkage (as a rule-of-thumb, at ϵ-shrinkage $> 5\%$ this plot loses informativeness).[12] In cases of higher shrinkage, plots of CWRES versus individual predictions (IPRED), or $IWRES_{npde}$ [13] versus IPRED are more informative. The diagnostic plots as well as the significant drop in OFV indicate that the combined error model provides better fit.

Covariate model

The dataset *pktab1* contains three continuous covariates: weight (WT), creatinine clearance (CRCL), AGE, and two binary covariates: SEX and study center (CENT). Since the number of covariates is low (5), one might choose to test these covariates manually. However, in the next step of this tutorial we will perform stepwise covariate modeling (scm) in PsN, to demonstrate this automated method. In the first phase of the scm, covariates are added to the base model in a stepwise fashion based on statistical significance (decrease in OFV). In a second backward elimination phase, covariates are then removed from the final model obtained in the first phase, if removal of the covariate does not result in significantly worse fit. The backward step is typically done at a higher significance level. Like all PsN tools, the scm can be run from the command line or from Pirana, in a similar way as done before for execute. However, the scm tool requires that a configuration file is created first. Several examples of configuration files are available on the PsN website, but here we will create one using the wizard in Pirana (*Tools → Wizards → scm configuration file*). Create a configuration file, with the filename (psp.scm), in which all covariates are tested on both CL and V1, at a significance level of 0.1 (forward step) and 0.05 (backward step) and restrict the analysis to linear relationships (set the relationships argument to 1,2). Check that the correct covariates are included; the ones shown in the wizard are only placeholders. If youre not sure on the correct syntax of the scm file, please have a look at the provided annotated configuration file (psp.scm in the on-line appendix). Before starting the scm, duplicate run3.mod to run4.mod, and remove any $TABLE records that are present. Start the scm from the PsN dialog window using this command:

```
scm psp.scm model =run4.mod
```

After the scm has completed, PsN will compile an output file called *scmlog.txt* in the scm folder. Open this file and interpret the information, it holds the results for all tests performed in the scm and shows how the final covariate model was constructed. You should find that 4 covariate relationships are significant: CRCL on CL, WT on CL, WT on V, and SEX on V. This will be our final model from the covariate model-building step. If you did not find these results, compare your results with those provided in the on-line appendix.

More elaborate covariate model building techniques based on the scm are available in PsN as well, such as the cross-validated scm (xv_scm)[14], and the bootstrap of the scm (boot_scm)[15]. These tools provide more details on the predictive ability of the model, and on selection bias and expected covariate model size, respectively. They can also be run on linearized versions of the model, to reduce the computational workload.[16] Other covariate modeling tools that are available in PsN include the lasso[17] and the fixed random effects model (FREM, [18]), while in Xpose the gam and bootstrap of the gam (bootgam) are implemented [6]. All of these methods have certain advantages and drawbacks, which are however beyond the scope of this article.

Final model

If the scm completed successfully, you will find a folder called *final_models* inside the scm folder created by PsN. Inside that folder, locate the final model with included covariate relations and copy that to the main model folder, renaming it to *run5.mod*. We will use this model to perform some more elaborate diagnostic evaluation, i.e. we will get bootstrap estimates for our parameters and create a VPC. So first open the PsN bootstrap dialog window (*Right click → PsN → Model diagnostic → bootstrap*). A required argument to the bootstrap command is the samples argument, which specifies how many bootstrap samples should be drawn. More samples will make the bootstrap estimates and percentile estimates more precise, however at the expense of increased computation times. The recommended number of samples for an analysis will depend on what statistic is desired by the modeler. For obtaining bootstrap means of the parameter estimates, 100 samples may be enough, but to obtain accurate 5th and 95th percentiles, 1,000 or more are required to obtain precise estimates. After the bootstrap is finished (on a single core, a bootstrap of 200 samples may easily take an hour for this model), the results from the bootstrap are available in the bootstrap folder, in the files *raw_results_run5.csv* and *bootstrap_results.csv*. Open these files and interpret the output: are the parameters estimated with adequate precision? In Pirana, select the bootstrap folder created by PsN and run the R-script to create plots of parameter distributions (*Scripts tab → PsN → Bootstrap results*), which facilitates evaluation and interpretation of these bootstrap results.

Earlier in this tutorial we presented how basic goodness-of-fit plots can be created in Pirana and Xpose. Now we will use all three tools to create a visual predictive check (VPC) of the final model (run5.mod).

A VPC is an internal validation tool, i.e. it shows how well the model predicts the data on which the model was conditioned. It visualizes the median model prediction, the variability between patients and within patients (5th and 95th percentiles), and the uncertainty around the predicted percentiles.[19] Before we create a VPC, we would like to stress a few points. Firstly, in VPCs it is important to show the uncertainty around the model predicted percentiles, instead of presenting only lines indicating the point estimates of the percentiles. Signs of model improvement are when the confidence areas of the simulated percentiles encompass more of the observation percentiles, but also when the confidence intervals themselves are shrinking (while still encompassing the observation percentiles). Furthermore, since the VPC shows summary statistics (percentiles) of observations and predictions for binned data, the binning method is an important consideration. To avoid inflation of the uncertainty around the summary statistics, each bin should contain an adequate amount of observations. A quick rule-of-thumb is that there should not be more bins than the number of observations per individual. PsN currently incorporates several binning approaches: manual bin specification (-bin_array=x,y,z,etc), binning into an equal number of datapoints per bin (-bin_by_count=1 no_of_bins=#), or spacing the bins equally over the x-axis (-bin_by_count=0, -no_of_bins=#). Importantly, binning across a large variability in dose and/or influential covariates can diminish the diagnostic value of a VPC. One approach to overcome this is to stratify the VPC by the covariate, but this is not always possible e.g. due to limited data per stratum. Also when data arises from studies with adaptive designs (e.g. dose adjustments), VPCs are misleading unless the adaptation protocol is included in the model. The prediction-corrected VPC (pcVPC) offers a solution to these problems while retaining the visual interpretation of the traditional VPC.[20] pcVPCs can be constructed by adding the argument pred_corr to the PsN VPC command.

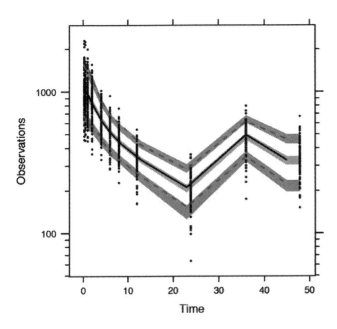

Figure 9.5: Visual Predictive Check (vpc)

VPCs can be made in Pirana using the PsN dialog window (*right click → PsN → model evaluation → VPC*), or from the command line. As discussed above, essential arguments to pass to the VPC are the number of samples and the binning method. Increasing the number of samples will increase the accuracy of the summary statistics for the simulation and their uncertainty interval (but it will not decrease the uncertainty interval itself). Start the VPC tool using:

```
vpc samples =500 no \_of\_bins=8 bin \_by\_count=1 run5.mod
```

The first of the two NONMEM runs that are started will only output a table with the necessary (observation) data for the VPC, it does not perform parameter estimation. The other model runs repeated Monte Carlo simulations of the model, using the same dataset design as the original. After the two NONMEM runs have finished, PsN will process the output, bin the simulated and observed data, calculate the percentiles and confidence intervals for each bin, and export a csv-file with the summary statistics. This csv-file can then be processed by Xpose and turned into a VPC-plot, which can be automated from Pirana using the Xpose GUI as described before, or using the R scripts library. Both approaches will create and open a pdf-file with the VPC (see example in figure 5). Using the latter approach this is done as follows: select the VPC-folder created by PsN, and open the Scripts tab on the right. In the list of R scripts, choose *Xpose* → *VPC* → *Basic_log_y.R*. A pdf-file with the VPC will be generated and opened from Pirana. As an exercise, try to create the same plot using the Xpose GUI in Pirana as well: select the model in the main overview, and *right click* → *Xpose* → *Xpose GUI*. Since only limited space is available for this tutorial we will not demonstrate other diagnostics. We will however create a run record of the model development: in the menu bar click *Results* → *Run records* → *Detailed run record (csv)*. This will create and open a csv-file containing run numbers, descriptions, other meta-information and run results. If the file does not open automatically, please look it up in the Files tab on the right and double click it. As a final step in our PK model development, select the final model again and bundle that model file, the associated result files and output files and the VPC folder into a zip-file (*Right click* → *File actions* → *Compress to zip-file*). Also create a bundled report of the goodness-of-fit plots for the final model (in the Reports tab select the desired pdfs and click *Bundle into...* → *<output format>*).

Additional features

For all three software tools presented here, we have only scratched the surface of possibilities. The reader is encouraged to explore more advanced functionality using the documentation available on the respective websites. We will highlight a few examples of more advanced features for the three programs below.

PsN the simulation and re-estimation (sse) tool can be used to evaluate trial designs, e.g. to evaluate whether model parameters can be estimated with adequate precision under the intended or alternative experimental designs or with alternative models. It is also useful for evaluating fundamental modeling aspects, e.g. to evaluate how model diagnostics perform under given designs. Another interesting tool for design evaluation, specifically for the calculation of study power and number of study subjects required, is Monte Carlo Mapped Power (mcmp).[21] In this tool, which is also based on simulation and re-estimation, the individual objective function values calculated in NONMEM are exploited to evaluate designs in a more rapid way than using sse. Case deletion diagnostics (cdd) is a tool that can be useful in the final stages of model development, to investigate whether model fit depends more heavily on particular strata of the dataset. The most important PsN functions are listed in table 3.

Xpose In this tutorial we showed how to create goodness-of-fit plots from the Xpose menu system, and from the Xpose interface in Pirana (VPC). However, the most efficient way to use Xpose, especially when doing repetitive jobs, is to use scripts to create the desired goodness-of-fit plots. A list of useful Xpose functions is given in table 2, while a more complete overview of functions and example scripts (bestiarium) is available on the Xpose website. The default plots in Xpose can be extended and modified in various ways. Firstly, most Xpose functions take arguments that alter the implementation of the plot. The looks of the plots can also be changed by directly passing lattice arguments to the Xpose function. Secondly, the input variables can be altered easily to allow creation of non-default plots. E.g. to create a plot of a covariate METAB vs IDV instead of DV vs IDV we can trick Xpose into using METAB as DV while maintaining the plot characteristics:

```
> change.xvardef(xpdb, "dv") <- c("METAB")
> xplot <- dv.vs.idv(xpdb)
> print(xplot)
```

Finally, since Xpose is an open source R module, it is possible to modify the Xpose functions directly, if further modifications are required.

Pirana a model translator is included that can translate any NON-MEM model (written in an NM-TRAN ADVAN subroutine), to differential equation code for R (using deSolve library), Berkeley Madonna (software dedicated to ODE simulations), or Matlab / PopED [22]. Note that many functions in Pirana can be extended and customized by the user, such as the R-scripts library and the wizards. Pirana can also be used for modeling on remote clusters (through ssh-connections), and has native support for SGE, Torque and Condor job schedulers.

Table 9.3: Commonly used PsN tools

Tool command	Description	Commonly used arguments
execute	Run a model in NONMEM	-retries picky model_dir_name
VPC	Visual predictive check	-samples -bin_by_count no_of_bins bin_array dv -idv
bootstrap	Run a bootstrap	-samples stratify_on
cdd	Case deletion diagnostics	-samples case_column
sse	Simulation and (re-)estimation	-samples alternative_models no-estimate_simulation
mcmp	Monte Carlo Mapped power	-n_bootstrap start_size increment -df
scm	Stepwise covariate modeling	-config_file model
xv_scm	Cross-validated stepwise covariate modeling	-config_file max_steps -splits
boot_scm	Bootstrap of stepwise covariate modeling	-config_file -samples dummy_covariates -run_final_models
llp	Log-Likelihood profiling and maximum-likelihood parameter estimates	-ofv_increase thetas omegas max_iterations
psn_options	Shows all general PsN options	
update_inits	Updates initial estimates based on a NONMEM output file from a previous run	-nm_version -verbose -from-model output_model
lasso	the Lasso (covariate modeling)	-relations lst_file
mimp	Multiple imputation (missing data method)	-base_model reg_model mi_model -imputations
General options*	Applies to every PsN tool	-clean

For each tool, the arguments h and help show a list of arguments and a detailed description of the arguments, respectively. Note that arguments can also be set in the psn configuration file. In that case they dont have to be specified again on the command line.

9.4 Conclusion

In this tutorial we presented a modeling workbench that incorporates three tools, which in our view make M&S with NONMEM more powerful, more efficient and easier to perform. It is our intention to implement all new modeling techniques and diagnostics developed within our group into PsN, Xpose and/or Pirana, so new versions are expected to be released on a regular basis.

Conflict of Interest

RJK is owner of Pirana Software & Consulting BV, which provides commercial licensing of Pirana. MOK and AH have no conflicts of interests.

Acknowledgements

The researchers in the Pharmacometrics Research Group are acknowledged for their input on the use of diagnostics in model development.

References

1. Sheiner LB, Beal SL. Evaluation of methods for estimating population pharmacokinetics parameters. I. Michaelis-Menten model: routine clinical pharmacokinetic data. Journal of pharmacokinetics and biopharmaceutics [Internet] 1980 [cited 2012 Aug 3];8(6):55371.

2. Stone JA, Banfield C, Pfister M, Tannenbaum S, Allerheiligen S, Wetherington JD, et al. Model-based drug development survey finds pharmacometrics impacting decision making in the pharmaceutical industry. Journal of clinical pharmacology [Internet] 2010 [cited 2012 Aug 3];50(9 Suppl):20S30S.

3. Zandvliet AS, Schellens JHM, Beijnen JH, Huitema ADR. Population pharmacokinetics and pharmacodynamics for treatment optimization in clinical oncology. Clinical pharmacokinetics [Internet] 2008 [cited 2012 Aug 3];47(8):487513.

4. Lindbom L, Pihlgren P, Jonsson EN, Jonsson N. PsN-Toolkit–a collection of computer intensive statistical methods for non-linear mixed effect modeling using NONMEM. Computer methods and programs in biomedicine [Internet] 2005 [cited 2012 Jul 25];79(3):24157.

5. Vlasakakis G, Comets E, Keunecke A, Gueorguieva I, Magni P, Terranova N, et al. White paper: Landscape on technical and conceptual requirements and competence framework in Drug / Disease Modeling & Simulation. CPT:PSP (In press)

6. Jonsson EN, Karlsson MO. Xpose–an S-PLUS based population pharmacokinetic/pharmacodynamic model building aid for NONMEM. Computer methods and programs in biomedicine [Internet] 1999 [cited 2012 Aug 3];58(1):5164.

7. Keizer RJ, Van Benten M, Beijnen JH, Schellens JHM, Huitema ADR. Piraa and PCluster: a modeling environment and cluster infrastructure for NONMEM. Computer methods and programs in biomedicine [Internet] 2011 [cited 2011 Jul 12];101(1):729.

8. Byon W, Smith MK, Chan P, Tortorici MA, Riley S, Dai H, et al. Establishing Best Practices and Guidance in Population Modeling: an Industry Experience with a Population Pharmacokinetic Analysis Guidance. CPT:PSP (In press)

9. Beal S, Sheiner LB, Boekmann A, Bauer RJ. NONMEMs User's Guides. Ellicott City, Maryland, USA.: ICON Development Solutions; 10. Hooker AC, Staatz CE, Karlsson MO. Conditional weighted residuals (CWRES): a model diagnostic for the FOCE method. Pharmaceutical research [Internet] 2007

10. Keizer RJ. The Visual Run Record: visualization of the model development history. In: Abstracts of the World Conference on Pharmacometrics. Seoul, South-Korea: 2012.

11. Karlsson MO, Savic RM. Diagnosing model diagnostics. Clinical pharmacology and therapeutics [Internet] 2007 [cited 2012 Aug 3];82(1):1720.

12. Keizer RJ, Harling K, Karlsson MO. Extended NPDE diagnostics for the between-subject variability and residual error model. PAGE. Abstracts of the Annual Meeting of the Population Approach Group in Europe. 2012;21:Abstr 2538.

13. Katsube T, Khandelwal A, Harling K, Hooker AC, Karlsson MO. Evaluation of Stepwise Covariate Model Building Combined with Cross Validation [Internet]. In. PAGE. Abstracts of the Annual Meeting of the Population Approach Group in Europe. 2011. page Abstr 2111.

14. Keizer RJ, Khandelwal A, Hooker AC, Karlsson MO. The bootstrap of stepwise covariate modeling. In: PAGE. Abstracts of the Annual Meeting of the Population Approach Group in Europe. Athens, Greece: 2011. page Abstr 2161.

15. Khandelwal A, Harling K, Jonsson EN, Hooker AC, Karlsson MO. A fast method for testing covariates in population PK/PD Models. The AAPS journal [Internet] 2011 [cited 2012 Aug 2];13(3):46472.

16. Karlsson MO. A full model approach based on the covariance matrix of parameters and covariates. PAGE. Abstracts of the Annual Meeting of the Population Approach Group in Europe. 2012;21:Abstr 2455.

17. A Tutorial on Visual Predictive Checks [Internet]. [cited 2012 Aug 3]; http://www.page-meeting.org/default.asp?abstract=1434

18. Bergstrand M, Hooker AC, Wallin JE, Karlsson MO. Prediction-corrected visual predictive checks for diagnosing nonlinear mixed-effects models. The AAPS journal [Internet] 2011 [cited 2012 Jul 17];13(2):14351.

19. Vong C, Bergstrand M, Nyberg J, Karlsson MO. Rapid sample size calculations for a defined likelihood ratio test-based power in mixed-effects models. The AAPS journal [Internet] 2012 [cited 2012 Aug 3];14(2):17686.

20. Nyberg J, Ueckert S, Strmberg EA, Hennig S, Karlsson MO, Hooker AC. PopED: An extended, parallelized, nonlinear mixed effects models optimal design tool. Computer methods and programs in biomedicine [Internet] 2012 [cited 2012 Aug 13]

Part III

Quick guides

9.5 Quick Guide: Configuring Pirana

Scope

This Pirana Quick Guide explains how to configure the most important settings in Pirana.

Most of the settings for Pirana can be configured through the menu File → Settings. The following sections deal with the different sections of the Settings window.

General settings

- The general settings window (Figure 1) deals with some of the general settings for working with Pirana.

- Most of settings do not need altering to work with Pirana. The meaning of most important settings is discussed below:

  Alternative data directory: Alternative location for model input data files.

  Enable nmfe runs: If this option is selected, models can be run directly using nmfe.

  Enable Pirana as wrapper for PsN/WFN/Monolix: If these options are selected, Pirana may be used to run models through PsN or WFN. Monolix support is experimental.

  Enable the use of PCluster: Experimental feature, not supported (refer to PC cluster manual).

NONMEM

- Refer to the NONMEM quick guide for detailed support on how to setup NONMEM instatllations.

- This is not necessery if PsN is used.

Software integration

- The software integration tab (Figure 2) deals with the integration of other software packages into Pirana.

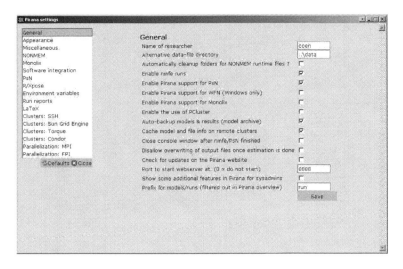

Figure 9.6: General settings window

- If the background of a software location appears green, the program can be found, whereas if it is red the program cannot be located under the specified path.

- Except for the list of programs defined below, *all other items in the software integration window are not necessery to define in order to work with Pirana*. Most other programs locations are only used to create easy links to the software from within Pirana. Also the location of *psn.conf* is not needed to work with PsN.

- The following software packages are important to set correctly in order to work with Pirana easily:

  R location; Pirana uses R and Xpose to generate graphs, hence it is important to set the path to R correctly.

  Location of R GUI (if available); if a GUI for R is available this should be specified. RStudio is recommended.

  Spreadsheet location (i.e. Excel, Numeric etc.), to view the contents of CSV files.

  Code/text editor; This editor will be used to edit models or scripts and is therefore important to define.

  PDF file viewer; Many graphics are created as PDF files, hence a PDF viewer is useful to define.

103

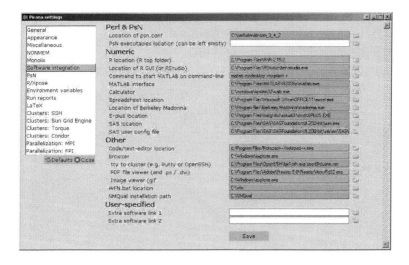

Figure 9.7: Software integration window

PsN

- Refer to PsN quick guide for detailed support on using PsN with Pirana.

- This settings window specified default command line parameters for PsN.

R/Xpose

- *Initialization commands* may be used to load specific R libraries when executing R/Xpose.

- *PDF/PNG/GIF/EPS Arguments*: Default plotting arguments for R printing devices.

- *Sweave preamble/postamble*: If the Sweave functionality from Xpose is used, the default LaTeX pre/postable may be specified here.

Clusters

- For more information on settings for clusters, please refer to the Clusters quick guide.

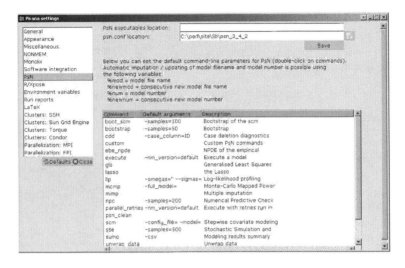

Figure 9.8: PsN settings window

Configure the Sun Grid Engine

- Defaults for working with SGE may be defined here.

Miscellaneous

- *File extensions*: File extensions are important to define because this wil determine if model files are shown (i.e. mod or ctl), and if NONMEM output files are correctly read (i.e. res or lst).

- *Linux*: Refers to defaults for terminal and shell

- *PCluster*: Settings for working with PCluster (unsupported, refer to PCluster manual).

- *NMQual settings*: Here, folders may be added to PATH or LIBRARY_PATH environmental variables.

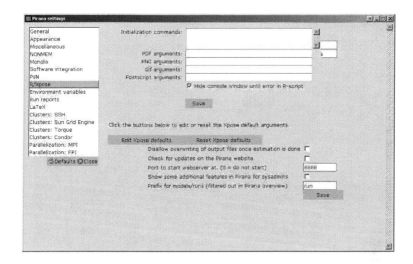

Figure 9.9: R/Xpose settings window

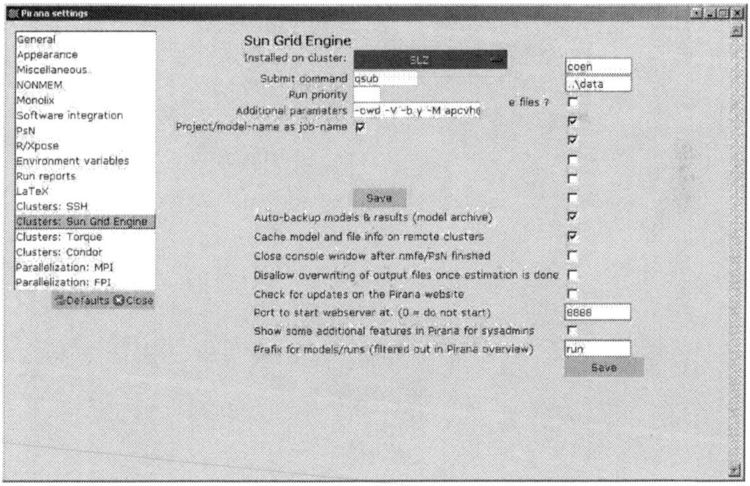

Figure 9.10: SGE

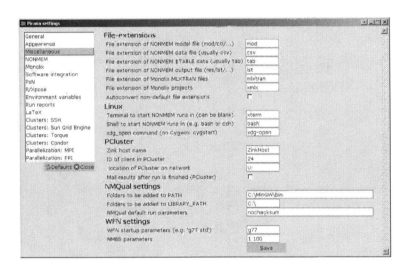

Figure 9.11: Miscellaneuous settings

9.6 Quick Guide: Setting up NONMEM in Pirana

Scope

This Pirana Quick Guide explains how add NONMEM (nmfe) installations to Pirana. This procedure is not required for PsN installations, which are automatically recognized if PsN is configured appropriately. It will also be discussed how to set up installations that use Intel Fortran v11 as compiler within Pirana. Note: in this quick guide it will be assumed that you already have installed NONMEM.

Add NONMEM installation setting window

- Go to File → Settings → NONMEM. The dialog window shown in Figure 1 appears.

- In this dialo, local (top part) and remote (bottom part) NON-MEM installations may be defined.

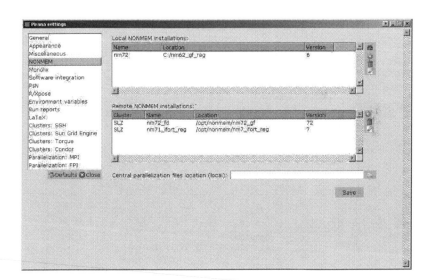

Figure 9.12: Adding a NONMEM installation

Adding local nonmem installations

- By pressing the Find icon (Figure 9.53, blue square), Pirana will automatically attempt to find any local NONMEM installations at common installation locations.

- If you installed NONMEM at a non-standard location and Pirana is not able to find it automatically, you will have to add it manually, by pressing the + button (Figure 9.53, red square).

- A window (Figure 9.54) will appear where the name and location of the NONMEM installation may be entered. The version of NONMEM will be automatically detected.

- After adding NONMEM installations, please press the Save button (Figure 9.53). The local NONMEM installations will then be available in Pirana.

Figure 9.13: Adding a local NONMEM installation

Adding remote nonmem installations

- Auto-detection of NONMEM installations is not available for remote NONMEM installations, they will have to be added manually.

- Press the + button next to *Remote NONMEM* installations, to add a remote installation.

- A window (Figure 9.55) appears, in which the installation name, the associated cluster, the location and the version can be defined.

- After adding NONMEM installations, press the Save button (Figure 9.53). The remote NONMEM installations are now available in Pirana.

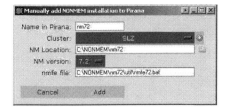

Figure 9.14: Adding a remote NONMEM installation

Using Intel Fortran 11 for Windows together with NONMEM/PsN

The Intel Fortran 11 compiler requires the user to set several environmental variables. If these variables are correctly defined system-wide, NONMEM installations using Intel Fortran should already work. However, if you are not able to set the environment variables system-wide, or you experience problems, you can also use Pirana to set them for you.

- Please refer to posts on NMusers (such as this one) where it is explained how environmental variables should be defined for Intel Fortran. These may differ slightly from system to system, so we can't give a fixed solution here. The common way in Windows to set these environment variables is by going to the Control panel → System settings → Environment variables. However, Pirana offers three alternative solutions to define the required environmental variables.

- The first option is through Tools → NONMEM → Environmental variables. Setting the environment variables here will set them prior to executing a model (nmfe-only).

- The second option is through File → Settings → Software integration → 'Add this to path at Pirana startup. Note that this only adds locations to the PATH environment variable. Most likely, you will have to set a few more environment variables as well.

- The last option is by adding a text file add_env.txt or set_env.txt to the main Pirana folder. These text files can be used to *add* to or *set* any environmental variables. These files could for instance look as below.

110

```
PATH=C:\nmvi\run;C:\MinGW\bin
LIB=C:\Program files\Intel
fortran\bin
```

9.7 Quick Guide: Setting up cluster connections

Scope

This Pirana Quick Guide explains how to prepare, configure and work with a cluster over SSH, and how to subsequently work with Pirana to execute models on the cluster.

Preparation: SSH access

In order to execute runs on a cluster from a local system with Pirana, SSH access to the cluster from your local computer must be available.

- For Windows, the easiest way to do this is to install Putty. Make sure that you install the complete version of PuTTY, including the command line tool *plink.exe*.

- After installation, make sure Putty is available in the system path, or add the location of the Putty folder to the internal Pirana path via File $\rightarrow$ Settings $\rightarrow$ Software integration $\rightarrow$ 'Add this folder(s) to PATH at Pirana startup'.

- On Linux and Mac OSX, ssh is most likely already installed.

Preparation: Mounting a cluster folder as local drive

A remote folder on the cluster should be mounted as a local drive letter (e.g. R:) on your system. There are several ways to do this, some of which are described below. Please check with your system administrator if you don't manage to mount the cluster as a local drive.

- If the cluster is running Samba, a drive letter may be mounted through My Computer $\rightarrow$ Extra $\rightarrow$ Network connections.

- If only SSH (SFTP) access is available, software such as Expandrive may be considered.

Configuring the cluster

If the remote cluster folder can be mounted as drive letter on your system, and you have installed putty, cluster access may now be configured in Pirana.

112

- Access the settings menu via File → Settings → Clusters. A screen is obtained as depicted in Figure 9.53.

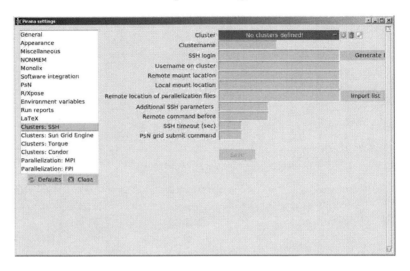

Figure 9.15: Cluster settings window

- Select the + sign to add a new cluster. Some initial settings are pre-entered in the textboxes of the newly defined cluster (Figure 9.54), but these have to be updated to match your cluster.

- In the textbox *Clustername*, define a name for the cluster (can be anything).

- The textbox *SSH login* should contain the command to connect to the cluster. If Putty is used, this command will start with *plink*, followed by the user name, password and name or IP address of the cluster access node, e.g. 'plink -l myname -p mypassw pkpd.server.org'. Passwordless access using a RSA key is also possible.

- The textbox *Remote mount location* refers to a folder on the cluster which you have mounted as local drive.

- The textbox *Local mount location* should contain the drive-letter on the local system which corresponds with the remote cluster path defined in the previous textbox.

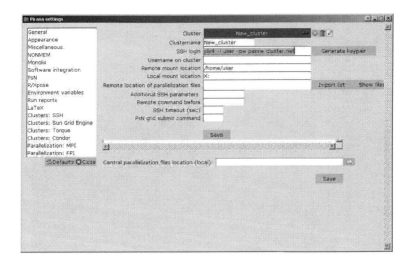

Figure 9.16: Pre-entered text after adding a new cluster

- In the following textboxes, *Additional SSH parameters*, and *Remote commands before* connecting to the cluster, and the *PsN grid submit command* may be defined, but these are not required.

- An example of a fully configured cluster is depicted in Figure 9.55.

Working with the cluster

- Any runs which are to be submitted to the cluster should be in a location on the drive which you specified the remote cluster mount location.

- A model can be run on the cluster via either *nmfe* or *PsN*, which are described separately below.

Submitting a run to the cluster via nmfe

- When submitting a run via nmfe, after selecting a model and opening the 'nmfe'-run dialog, select a cluster to connect to (Figure 9.56, blue quare).

114

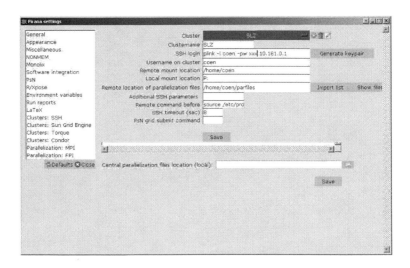

Figure 9.17: Settings of a fully configured cluster

- The option *Submit to [..]* should be selected if the run is to be submitted to a job scheduler. (Figure 9.56, green square). Currently supported schedulers are Sun Grid Engine (SGE), Torque and Condor.

- Optionally, for NONMEM 7.2, parallalization files may be selected.

- Start the run.

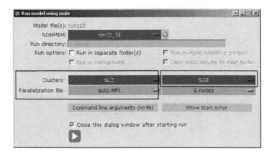

Figure 9.18: Defining cluster settings for a nmfe run

Submitting a run to the cluster via PsN

- Select a cluster for the PsN run (Figure 5, orange square).

- Add optional arguments to the PsN argument, such as *-run_on_sge*, if the run is submitted to SGE (Figure 9.57, red square).

- Several PsN arguments are available for other job schedulers such as LSF (Figure 9.57, blue square). Please note that the configuration of these job schedulers should be done in the psn.conf file on the cluster. Please refer to the PsN manual for more information about this.

- Start the run.

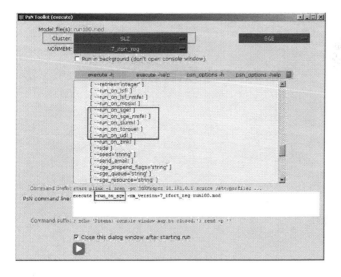

Figure 9.19: Defining cluster settings for a PsN run

Monitoring jobs on a SGE cluster

- If SGE, Torque or Condor is used as job managment system, the queue may be monitored using the integrated monitor in Pirana.

- This feature may be accessed by clicking the SGE icon in the main Pirana interface (Figure 9.54, red square).

- In the interface that is opened, an overview will be presented of the jobs that are currently running, scheduled, or have recently been finished. Some information about available nodes in the SGE cluster can also be viewed.

- By right-clicking on a job, you can view more information about it, or kill it. Please note that not only NONMEM jobs are shown here, but any compute job (e.g. MATLAB).

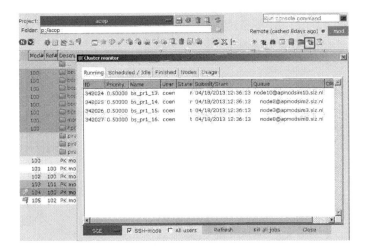

Figure 9.20: Cluster run window

9.8 Quick Guide: Working with models

Introduction

- All models and their associated results available in a folder in Pirana are depicted in the main Window.

- When selecting a model and using the right mouse-button menu, a range of actions may be performed on the selected model.

- Most manipulations (duplicating, removing, etc.) of models are available via the sub-menu *Actions* (Figure 9.53).

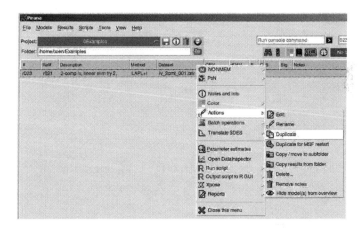

Figure 9.21: Pirana window with context menu

Running a model

- Select the model and open the right-mouse button context menu.

- Select the preferred methode of running the model, i.e. NON-MEM → nmfe, or PsN → execute.

- If you are using nmfe to run a model, NONMEM has to be registered within Pirana first (refer to the Quick Guide on installing NONMEM). If PsN is installed, Pirana will automatically recognize this.

Running a model using nmfe

After having selected Run via nmfe, the Run window depicted in Figure 9.54 will appear. A number of options are available here, before executing the run.

- *NONMEM*: The preferred NONMEM installations may be selected.

- *Run in seperate folder(s)*: A NONMEM run may be executing in a sub-folder, to enable to run multiple runs simultaneously. Results from a subfolder can be imported to the main folder in Pirana.

- *Run in background*: No console window is opened, the model is run in the background.

- *Clusters-Submit to SGE*: Run on a cluster using SGE (optional).

- *Clusters-Parallelization*: Run using parallelization available in NON-MEM 7.2 (optional).

- *Connect to*: Cluster (optional). Connect to a cluster. Please refer to the Quick Guide on Clusters for more information.

- *Script contents*: The script which is executed to run the model.

- The run may be executed using the > button.

Running a model using PsN

After having selected Run via PsN, the PsN run window depicted in Figure 9.55 will appear. Again, a number of options are available here, before executing the run.

- *Cluster*: Cluster to connect to (optional). Please refer to the Quick Guide on Clusters for more information.

- *NONMEM*: The preferred NONMEM installations may be selected.

- *Run in background*: After executing the model, output is not printed to the screen.

- *PsN command line*: This is the command line which is executed. Additional PsN arguments may be added here.

119

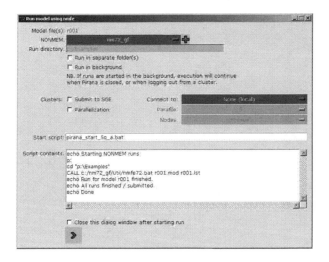

Figure 9.22: Run window for nmfe

- The top part of the window shows an overview for of available PsN arguments.

Generating an empty control stream

- An empty control stream may be generated via Models → New model (Figure 9.56).

- Choose the template control stream that you want to use.

- The control stream will be opened in the text editor defined in Settings.

Generating a new control stream using the Wizard

- Empty, partly pre-coded PK models may be generated using the Wizard (Tools → Wizards).

- In the Wizards menu (Figure 9.57), select PK NONMEM model.

- After finishing the Wizard, a new control stream will be created and opened in the editor.

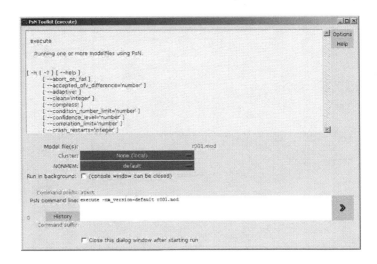

Figure 9.23: Run window for PsN

Editing a control stream

- A control stream visible in the main Pirana window may be edited by double clicking on the model.

- Alternatively, this may be done through the right-mouse button menu Actions → Edit.

- Please note that an alternative code editor can be defined through File → Settings → Software integration. The default in Pirana is notepad.exe, but it is highly recommended to change this to an appropriate code editor such as Emacs, ConText, or PSPad.

Duplicating a control stream

- A control stream may be duplicated through the right-mouse button menu Actions → Duplicate (Figure 9.53).

- In the resulting Duplication window (Figure 9.44), you can choose to update parameter estimates in the new file to the ones estimated for the current model, fix the parameter estimates, change the file numbers in $TABLE and $EST records.

- Please note that to correctly duplicate with updated parameter estimates, you are required to adhere to some coding guide-

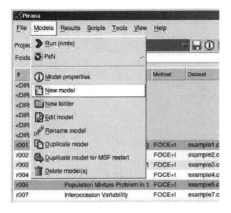

Figure 9.24: Create an empty model

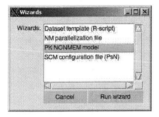

Figure 9.25: Create a new model using the Wizard

lines, especially for the $OMEGA and $SIGMA blocks. See the Pirana manual for more information.

- After pressing the Duplicate button, a new model will be created and opened in the editor.

Renaming a control stream

- A control stream may be renamed through the right-mouse button menu Actions → Rename (Figure 9.53). Some of the same options as under duplication are available.

Deleting a control stream

- A control stream may be deleted by selecting the right-mouse button menu Actions → Delete (Figure 9.53). Alternatively, a

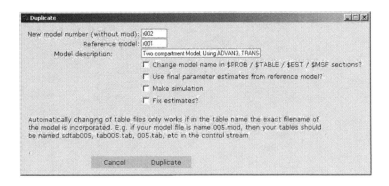

Figure 9.26: Create a new model using the Wizard

can be selected and subsequently the keyboard button DELETE can be pressed.

- In the dialog that is opened, you can select what to delete: only the control stream (models), or also the associated results files, datasets. If you have selected one or more folders in the main overview to be deleted, the 'folder' option should be checked to actually delete these as well.

Viewing parameter estimates inside the GUI

- During model building, parameter estimates can be viewed by selecting a run, and opening the Estimates Tab on the right panel (Figure 9.45).

- The parameter estimates window can be opened from the option Parameter estimates in the context menu (right mouse button) (Figure 9.28), or alternatively from the button in the right panel with estimates.

- Results from the table can be exported to CSV, LaTeX or HTML, and different transformations of variances can be selected.

- When selecting multiple runs, parameter estimates can be compared with each other (Figure 9.29).

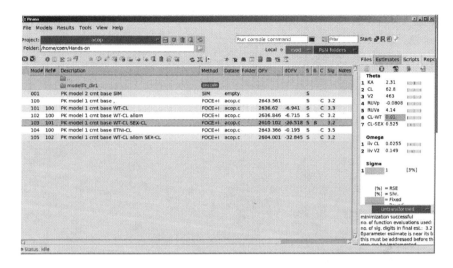

Figure 9.27: Viewing estimates in right panel in the Pirana GUI

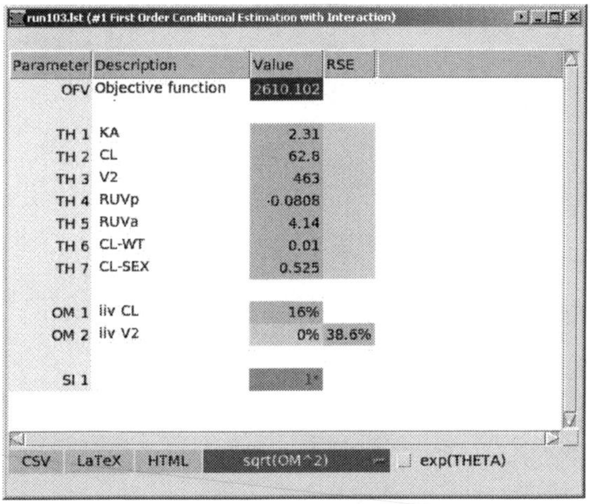

Figure 9.28: Parameter estimates window

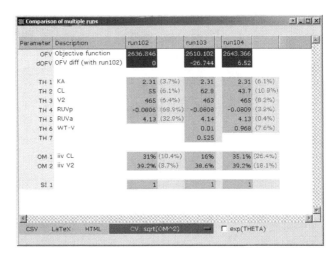

Figure 9.29: Parameter estimates comparison

9.9   Quick Guide: Creating reports

Scope

This Pirana Quick Guide aims to provide an overview of current reporting functionality available in Pirana.

Overview of functionality

The following functionality for reporting is available in Pirana:

- Run reports in various formats (HTML, Word, text, LaTeX, pdfLaTeX)

- Run records of multiple runs (CSV/Excel, HTML, Word, text)

- Visual interactive run records.

- Execution log files of executed runs.

Generating run reports

- From the menu or context menu, the option Reports can be accessed, which allows generation of various run reports (Figure 9.56) of one or more runs (if more runs are selected simultaneously).

- The components to be included in the report can be modified (Reports menu, option "Include in reports")

- Generated run reports are placed into a pirana_reports folder, and can be accessed from the tab Reports in the right panel of Pirana (Figure 9.57).

Generating run records

- Run records are documents that contain reports (e.g. as above) for all runs in the project folder.

- Run records can be created under Results → Run records.

- The CSV run record is a CSV file that can be opened in excel containing a table of all results (e.g. description, OFV, estimates, RSEs etc) for each model.

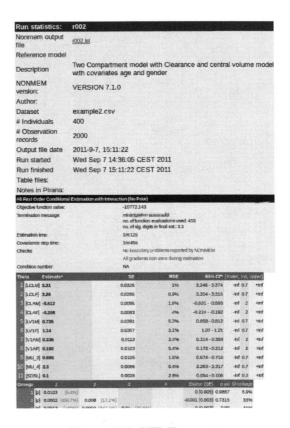

Figure 9.30: HTML report

Generating a visual run record

- The visual run record (VRR) is a SVG file which contains an interactive tree view of the model development process (Figure 9.44.

- Models are related to each other based on Pirana's reference model tags in the model file.

- The visual run record can be created under Results $\rightarrow$.

127

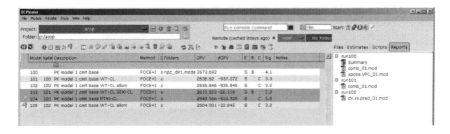

Figure 9.31: Overview of available reports in right panel

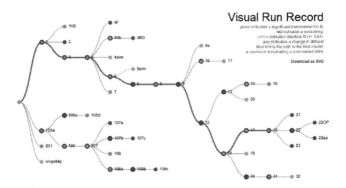

Figure 9.32: Visual run record

9.10 Quick Guide: Graphical output in R

Scope

This Pirana Quick Guide explains how to use Pirana to generate and modify diagnostic graphs using the integrated R scripts library.

Pirana has an integrated library of R scripts which can be used to generate diagnostic plots based on model output files. The library of R scripts can also be easily edited or extended with new scripts.

Creating diagnostic plots

- Select the model for which you want to create plots.

- In the right panel under Scripts, select the desired script.

- Via the context menu, select run script. clicking the right mouse button, and then selecting 'Run script', and subsequently selecting the plot you want to create (Figure 9.53).

- The plot will be created and openened automatically (Figure 9.54).

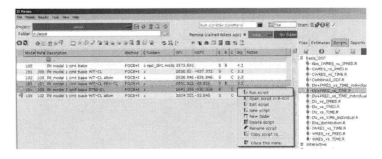

Figure 9.33: Running a script on a model run

Troubleshooting problems with plot creation

- If an error occurs, the R output will be displayed, which can be used to diagnose the error (Figure 9.55).

129

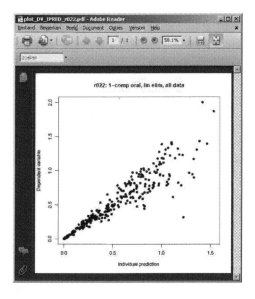

Figure 9.34: Diagnostic plot created

- Most frequently this is due to a variable missing in the output table files (e.g. column IPRED not available in output table).

- The expected input variables for each script are depicted at the bottom of the right panel.

Customizing diagnostic plots

- Instead of running the script through Run Script (above), the script may also be outputted to the R GUI ("Output script to R GUI") (Figure 9.56). Now, you can easily tweak the plot, and save it in the format you like.

- Afrter sending the script to R GUI, it will be opened there, where it may be further modified. Next, the script can be executed and the plot will be created within the R GUI (Figure 5).

Editing and creating scripts

- When one whishes to permanently make changes to the scripts library, this can be done using the option "Edit script" in the

```
> setwd('p:/Examples')
> model_names <- names(models)
> if (!file.exists("pirana_temp")) (dir.create ("pirana_temp"))
> if (file.exists (paste("pirana_temp/plot_DV_IPRED_",names(models)[1],".pdf", sep="")))(
+    file.remove (paste("pirana_temp/plot_DV_IPRED_",names(models)[1],".pdf", sep=""))
+ )
> pdf (file = paste("pirana_temp/plot_DV_IPRED_",names(models)[1],".pdf", sep=""))
> for (i in 1:length(model_names)) (
+    mod       <- models[[model_names[i]]]
+    tab_file <- mod$tables[1]
+    if (file.exists (tab_file)) (
+       tab       <- read.table (tab_file, skip=1, header=T) # NONMEM table with ONEHEADER option
+       if ("MDV" %in% names(tab)) ( tab <- tab[tab$MDV==0,] )
+       if ("EVID" %in% names(tab)) ( tab <- tab[tab$EVID==0,] )
+       colnames(tab)[match ("IPRE", names(tab))] <- "IPRED"
+       not.found <- req.fields[is.na(match(req.fields, colnames(tab)))]
+       if ( length (not.found) > 0) (
+          cat (paste("The variable(s)",not.found,"were not found. Please check your output tables.
+          quit()
+       )
+       plot (x=tab$IPRE, tab$DV, main = paste (model_names[i],": ", mod$description, sep=""),
+             pch=19, xlab="Individual prediction", ylab="Dependent variable")
+    )
+ )
> dev.off()
null device
          1
>
> print (paste("$", "PIRANA_OUT ","pirana_temp/plot_DV_IPRED_",names(models)[1],".pdf", sep=""))
[1] "$PIRANA_OUT pirana_temp/plot_DV_IPRED_r022.pdf"
Pirana: Trying to load file pirana_temp/plot_DV_IPRED_r022.pdf
>
> quit()
```

Figure 9.35: Output of the script

right panel context menu. (Figure 9.44).

- Any changes made to the script will be saved permanently. You can choose to make changes in the script that are originally supplied with Pirana, or have them in your own user library.

- Script files are located either in the user folder (e.g. C:\Documents and Settings\Username \.pirana\scripts), or in the main Pirana folder (e.g. C:\Program Files\Pirana). The organization of scripts in sub-menus is according to the folder structure in these scripts folders (Figure 9.45), and can be adjusted accordingly.

- Note that when you install a new version of Pirana over the old one, any R script you have in the Pirana folder will be overwritten with the one supplied by the new version of Pirana (if you haven't given the R-script another name).

- Through the menu 'Scripts' → 'New scripts', it is also possible to define new scripts. Please note that at current, you will have to restart Pirana for the script to show up in the interface.

131

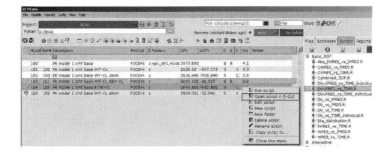

Figure 9.36: Output of a script to the R GUI for further customization

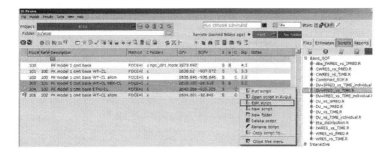

Figure 9.37: Editing templates for scripts

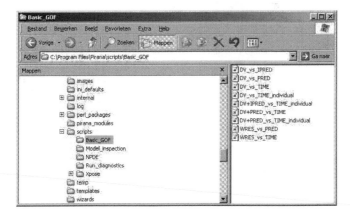

Figure 9.38: Script files present in the scripts sub-folder of Pirana

9.11 Quick Guide: Creating a VPC

Scope

This Pirana Quick Guide explains how to use Pirana to generate VPC data using PsN, and how to subsequently use that data to create VPC plots with Xpose using different plotting options.

Generating data for the VPC

- Select the model for which a VPC should be created, and select the option VPC via the menu below your right-mouse button (PsN → Model evaluation → vpc) (Figure 9.53).

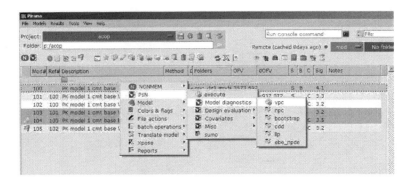

Figure 9.39: Selecting a run and executing the PsN/VPC Toolkit run window

- In the resulting PsN settings window, the command for running creating the vpc can be specified (Figure 9.54). The vpc command takes many arguments which alters the way the vpc is calculated, e.g. you can specify stratifications, binning, dependent variable etc.

- Arguments may be added in the text box at the lower part of the PsN run window (orange square). Make sure to separate the arguments by a space, and start each argument with a '-'.

- A full overview of possible arguments and their use may be viewed in the upper part of the PsN run window. By clicking on

133

'Help', additional help on these arguments is available (small blue square).

- When all arguments for the VPC dataset have been defined correctly, the PsN/vpc run may be executed (green square).

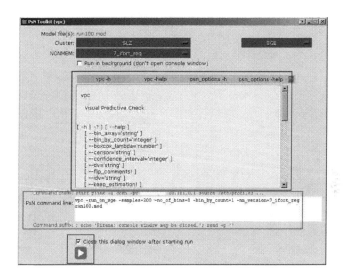

Figure 9.40: PsN/vpc Toolkit run window

- If the VPC run is not executed in the background, a run window will appear similiar to Figure Figure 9.55. Make sure to check if no errors are reported in this step. If the vpc finishes correctly, it will report something like 'Done reading and formatting data, finishing run.'

Figure 9.41: Output after execution of VPC run using PsN

Plotting the VPC data

- If the VPC was run succesfull, a new folder will be created which is named npc_dirX, at least if you did not specify another folder name manually (Figure 9.55, blue square).

- If you don't see the folder yet in Pirana, press the folder refresh button (round green/white button). Also make sure that the folder filter is set to *PsN folders* or *All folders* (Figure 9.55, orange square).

- Note that if you run the vpc command multiple times, multiple *npc_dir* folders will be created. It is therefore advisable to use the '-dir' option in PsN to specify a specific folder each time you run a vpc.

Figure 9.42: VPC run folder created after execution of VPC run

- Select the model for which the VPC was executed. (Figure 9.57).

- Select Xpose → Run Xpose commands. This will open up the Pirana Xpose interface.

- Enter or select xpose.VPC in the command text field (Figure 9.44, blue square). If any other commands are present in the list, remove these.

- Next, arguments for the Xpose.VPC may be added (Figure 9.44, orange square). The xpose.VPC help files may be accessed using the help button.

- Several options are available for the output format. The easiest option is to automatically generate the graph and save as PDF (default) or PNG file (Figure 9.44, red square).

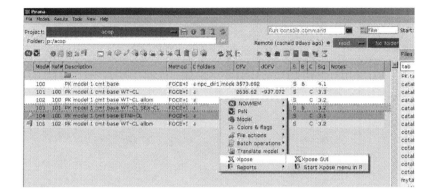

Figure 9.43: Starting the 'Run Xpose commands' window on selected run.

- Alternative output formats are to generate the R-code only and open it in your R interface, or to to generate Sweave code for LaTeX documents.

- If all settings have been configured, the VPC may be generated by pressing the execute button (Figure 9.44, green square).

- If output was directed to a PDF or PNG file, this file will be automatically opened by the PDF viewer you specified in Pirana's settings. (Figure 9.45). If you choose to generate R or LaTeX code, Pirana will open the R GUI or your code editor, and you will have to run the generated code manually.

Tweaking the VPC plot

These VPCs may be further optimized by adjusting the many Xpose arguments. Please check out the xpose VPC help files (which may be accessed from the Run Xpose command window, or go the the Xpose website for more information).

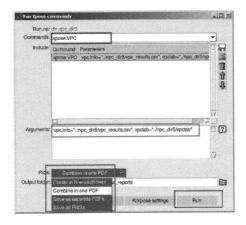

Figure 9.44: The 'Run Xpose commands' window to generate the VPC graph

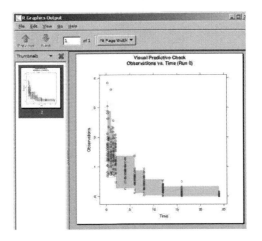

Figure 9.45: VPC obtained through PsN and Xpose

9.12 Quick Guide: Using Xpose from Pirana

Scope

This Pirana Quick Guide explains how to use Pirana to generate diagnostic graphs using Xpose. Please note that a separate Quick Guide describes how to create VPCs in PsN / Xpose.

Generating appropriate NONMEM output tables for Xpose

- Before Xpose diagnostic graphics can be generated, the model first needs to be executed while generating output tables in a specific format and naming.

- Briefly, for a controlstream named run10.mod, output tables such as sdtab10 (observations/predictions), patab10 (parameters), cotab10 (continuous covariates), and catab10 (categorical covariates) should be generated, with the NOPRINT and ONE-HEADER options.

- For more information on how to generate Xpose-ready $TABLE output files, please refer to the Xpose manual.

Generating Xpose graphs using the integrated Pirana menu

- Select the preferred run and select Xpose from the right mouse-button menu, and subsequently 'Run Xpose commands' (Figure 9.53).

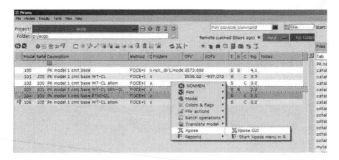

Figure 9.46: Selecting a run and executing the Rub Xpose commands winow

- In the dialog window that is opened, different Xpose graphs may be selected and defined (Figure 9.54).

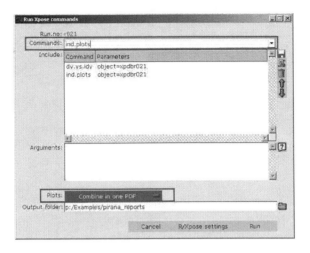

Figure 9.47: Run Xpose commands window

- From the *Commands menu* (red square), *multiple* Xpose plots may be added to the included list of Xpose plots.

- Additional *Arguments* may be specified for each Xpose command. A reference to possible arguments is provided under the ? sign.

- Several options are available for the output format of the *Plots*. The easiest option is to automatically generate the graph and save as PDF (default) or PNG file.

- If multiple Xpose graphs are selected, these will be appended in the output file (except PNG).

- Alternative output formats of the plots are to generate the R-code only, or to to generate Sweave code for LaTeX documents.

- If all settings have been configured, the plot(s) may be generated by pressing the execute button (>).

- If output was directed to a PDF file, the PDF will be opened automatically once it is generated (Figure).

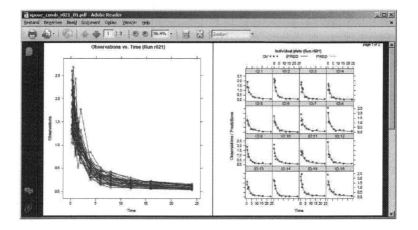

Figure 9.48: Xpose graphs in output PDF file

- Lists of commands can be saved and loaded from this dialog as well. This can be useful e.g. for standardized report generation.

Generating Xpose graphs using the conventional menu in R

- Alternatively, it is possible to automatically open the text-based Xpose menu in R from within Pirana.

- Select the preferred run and select Xpose from the right mouse-button menu, and subsequently ' Start Xpose menu' (Figure 1).

- The Xpose menu will now be started in R and the associated table files will be loaded into Xpose, from where graphs may be generated.

9.13 Quick Guide: Translating NM-TRAN

Scope

This Pirana Quick Guide explains how blocks of differential equations defined in $DES can be converted to differential equations code that can be used for simulation using R/de-Solve, Berkeley Madonna or Matlab.

Introduction

- If a model contains differential equations as defined in a $DES-block, these may be converted to R/deSolve, Berkeley Madonna or Matlab.

- This can be done by selecting a model, accessing the right-mouse-button menu and then selecting *Translate Model* (Figure 9.53).

- Next, files will be generated containing code to numerically solve these differential equations. The code can be used to perform simulations in these software packages.

- Pirana will automatically extract parameter values and use them in the simulation code. If the selected model has already been run in NONMEM, it will use the final parameter estimates. If a result file is not available, Pirana will use the initial parameter estimates. Note that parameter esimates are extracted for fixed effects only.

- Generated R/deSolve code will be automatically loaded in the defined R interface. Berkeley Madonna and Matlab code will be opened in the defined code editor. Examples of generated R and Berkeley Madonna code are depicted in Figures 9.54 and 9.55 respectively.

- An example of associated simulation output for the R/deSolve code is depicted in Figure 9.56.

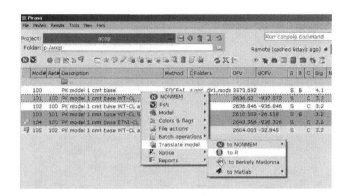

Figure 9.49: Translate options in Pirana

Figure 9.50: Generated BM code

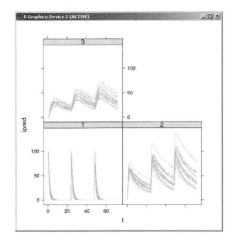

Figure 9.51: Generated R code

```
### Pirana generated deSolve code (PDK2011)
### Number of ODEs in system : 7
library (deSolve)
library (MASS)
library (lattice)

### Dose and Time Settings
A_init     <- c(0,0,0)  # Initial state of ODE system
n_doses    <- 3
dose_cmt   <- 1
ii         <- 24
dose_times <- seq (from = 0, by=ii, to=n_doses*ii)
dose_amts  <- c(rep (100, n_doses), 0)
times      <- seq(from=0, to=ii*n_doses, by=.5)  # Integration window and steps
obs_c      <- c(1:3)  # Observation compartments
n_ind      <- 20
n_par      <- 10

### Parameters
theta <- c(0.189, 2.86, 0.641, 2.03, 0.569, 0.865)
omega <- diag(.04, n_par)  # 10% ii- in each parameter
etas  <- mvrnorm(n = n_ind, mu=rep(0, n_par), Sigma=omega )

draw_params <- function (eta) {
    p <- list()  # parameter list
    p$CL  <- theta[1]  * exp(eta[1])
    p$VC  <- theta[2]  * exp(eta[2])
    p$Q   <- theta[3]  * exp(eta[3])
    p$VP  <- theta[4]  * exp(eta[4])
    p$K   <- p$CL/p$VC
    p$K12 <- p$Q/p$VC
    p$K21 <- p$Q/p$VP
    p$F1  <- theta[5]  * exp(eta[5])
    p$KA  <- theta[6]  * exp(eta[6])
    return(p)
}

### ODE system
-:--- 001 odesolve.R    Top L1    (ESS[S] [none])------------------------------
```

Figure 9.52: Graphical output of simulation R code

143

9.14 Quick Guide: Using PsN from Pirana

Scope

This Pirana Quick Guide explains how to use Pirana to work with the modeling toolkit Perl speaks NONMEM (PsN). This freely available toolkit is developed by Uppsala University and extends the funtionality of NONMEM with many tools, e.g. for advanced execution of models, performing bootstraps of model estimations, stepwise covariate modeling, log-likelihood profiling, stochastic simulation and (re-)estimation, and many more. PsN can also be used to generate various diagnostics, such as visual and numeric predictive checks (VPC / NPC).

Note: this is not a guide to PsN itself. If you have questions on the use of PsN, please check the PsN manual or contact the developers of PsN at http://psn.sourceforge.net.

Introduction / Setting up PsN

- If you haven't installed PsN, download the latest version from http://psn.sourceforge.net, and follow the instructions.

- The most important part after installation is to make sure that PsN knows where NONMEM is installed. PsN can do this for you automatically during the installation.

- To configure NONMEM installations manually for PsN, look up the file **psn.conf** in the folder where PsN was installed (on Windows probably somewhere in C:\Perl\site\PsN_x_x_x. (Note that an alternative psn.conf can be created in your home folder which overrides the system-wide psn.conf.) Open the configuration file in a text editor (e.g. notepad), and scroll to the section **[nm_versions]**, an example is shown in Figure 9.53

- In this **[nm_versions]** section you should define where NONMEM versions are installed on your system, and which version. Follow the comments and examples that are given in the PsN website if you are not sure what to put here.

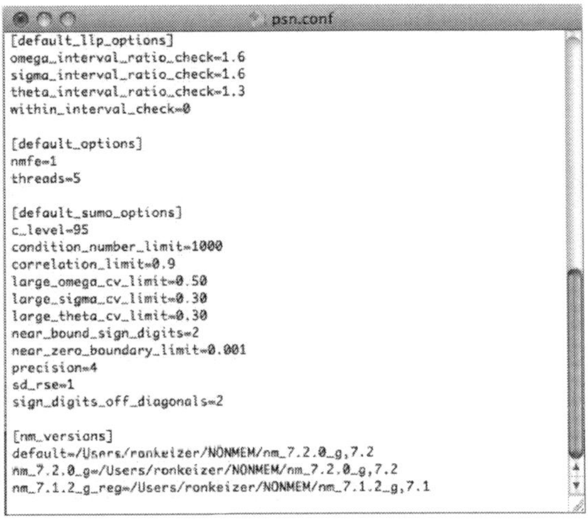

```
[default_llp_options]
omega_interval_ratio_check=1.6
sigma_interval_ratio_check=1.6
theta_interval_ratio_check=1.3
within_interval_check=0

[default_options]
nmfe=1
threads=5

[default_sumo_options]
c_level=95
condition_number_limit=1000
correlation_limit=0.9
large_omega_cv_limit=0.50
large_sigma_cv_limit=0.30
large_theta_cv_limit=0.30
near_bound_sign_digits=2
near_zero_boundary_limit=0.001
precision=4
sd_rse=1
sign_digits_off_diagonals=2

[nm_versions]
default=/Users/ronkeizer/NONMEM/nm_7.2.0_g,7.2
nm_7.2.0_g=/Users/ronkeizer/NONMEM/nm_7.2.0_g,7.2
nm_7.1.2_g_reg=/Users/ronkeizer/NONMEM/nm_7.1.2_g,7.1
```

Figure 9.53: Edit PsN configuration file

Using the execute command

- First, we will show how the PsN *execute* command can be used from Pirana.

- Select a model that you want to run in NONMEM, right-click with the mouse in the model overview, and select **PsN → execute**. This will bring up the PsN dialog for this command. Alternatively, you can use the Ctrl-E shortcut to do this. Now you will see the following window:

- The top part of this window shows the help file for this command. On the right-hand side you can choose whether you want to see the short help file only a list of the available arguments, or a long help file with explanations of the various arguments.

- In the text-box below, the actual PsN command can be typed. This will look something like:

```
execute -nm_version=default run1.mod
```

- To this command you can add arguments that you require. Many options are available, it is highly recommended to look into the

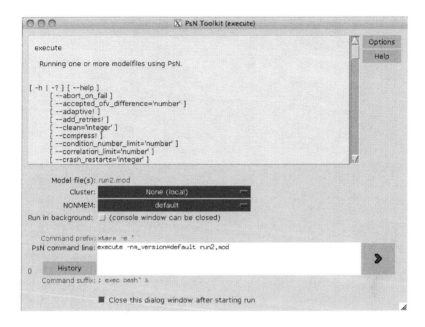

Figure 9.54: The PsN dialog in Pirana

available options. But for now let's just start the command like this. Pres the run button (¿), and Pirana will start the execute command, as shown in the screenshot below.

- What PsN actually does is create a subfolder in which the run is executed. After the NONMEM run finishes, PsN will copy back the results files to the main folder.

- Note that Pirana does not automatically detect that new results are available, so you should press the refresh button to load the results into the Pirana overview. To show the folders that PsN has created in the main overview, you have to select either 'PsN folders' or 'All folders' from the folder selection menu, highlighted below.

Using the other PsN tools

The other PsN tools are used in exactly the same way. For example to start a bootstrap, select a model and select 'bootstrap' from the PsN menu (under 'Model evaluation'), or using the Ctrl-B shortcut.

146

Figure 9.55: A PsN run in Windows (but run on a Linux cluster)

Make sure that at least the `-samples=`... argument is present in the command to be executed.

- You will notice that a 'History' button is present in the dialog as well. From the command list that is opened by clicking this button, you can select previously used PsN commands. Alternatively from the main PsN dialog you can also retrieve previously executed command by using Ctrl-up and Ctrl-down buttons.

- If there are special argument that you commonly use, you can set them as defaults. In Pirana, go to **Settings** → **PsN**. As shown in Figure 9.54 you can set here the default arguments for all PsN commands.

Using PsN data transformation tools

Besides tools for working with NONMEM executions, PsN also incorporates some tools to format or transform datasets, or display some statistics. To use these tools, go the file list on the right side of the Pirana window. Select a table or csv-file, and right click. From the menu select e.g. **PsN** → **data_stats**.

- A dialog window will now open, similar to the other PsN tools. You will notice that the **data_stats** tool only takes a few arguments.

- If you run this on a csv-file, In the console window that will be opened, some statistics are printed for each column in the dataset.

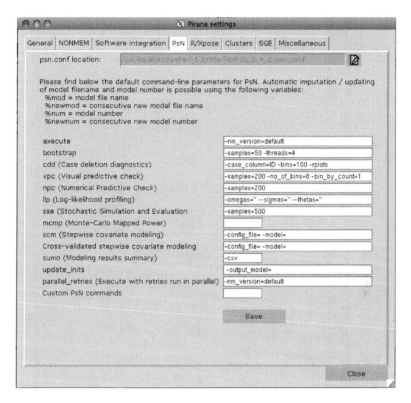

Figure 9.56: PsN default arguments in Pirana

- The other PsN dataset tools work in exactly the same way, although they perform conversions rather than printing information only.

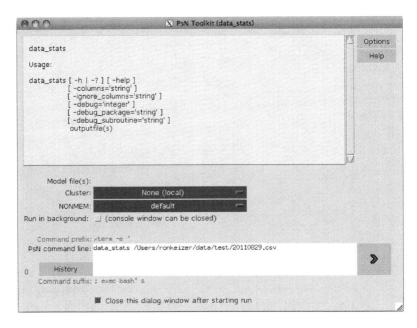

Figure 9.57: The PsN data_stats dialog in Pirana

Made in the USA
Monee, IL
27 November 2021

83192955R00088